Getting to
"Got It!"

ASCD MEMBER BOOK

Many ASCD members received this book as a
member benefit upon its initial release.

Learn more at: **www.ascd.org/memberbooks**

Getting to
"Got It!"

Helping Struggling Students
Learn How to Learn

Betty K. Garner

Association for Supervision and Curriculum Development
Alexandria, Virginia USA

Association for Supervision and Curriculum Development
1703 N. Beauregard St. • Alexandria, VA 22311-1714 USA
Phone: 800-933-2723 or 703-578-9600 • Fax: 703-575-5400
Web site: www.ascd.org • E-mail: member@ascd.org
Author guidelines: www.ascd.org/write

Gene R. Carter, *Executive Director;* Nancy Modrak, *Publisher;* Julie Houtz, *Director of Book Editing & Production;* Katie Martin, *Project Manager;* Reece Quiñones, *Senior Graphic Designer;* Keith Demmons, *Desktop Publishing Specialist;* Dina Murray Seamon, *Production Specialist/Team Lead*

Printed in the United States of America. Cover art copyright © 2007 by ASCD. ASCD publications present a variety of viewpoints. The views expressed or implied in this book should not be interpreted as official positions of the Association.

ASCD Member Book, No. FY08-2: (November 2007, PC). ASCD Member Books mail to Premium (P) and Comprehensive (C) members on this schedule: Jan., PC; Feb., P; Apr., PC; May, P; July, PC; Aug., P; Sept., PC; Nov., PC; Dec., P.

PAPERBACK ISBN: 978-1-4166-0608-6   ASCD product #107024
Also available as an e-book through ebrary, netLibrary, and many online booksellers (see Books in Print for the ISBNs).

Quantity discounts for the paperback edition only: 10–49 copies, 10%; 50+ copies, 15%; for 1,000 or more copies, call 800-933-2723, ext. 5634, or 703-575-5634. For desk copies: member@ascd.org.

Library of Congress Cataloging-in-Publication Data

Garner, Betty K., 1941–
  Getting to "Got it!" : helping struggling students learn how to learn / Betty K. Garner.
    p. cm.
  Includes bibliographical references and index.
  ISBN 978-1-4166-0608-6 (pbk. : alk. paper) 1. Learning. 2. Learning strategies. 3. Cognition in children. I. Title.
  LB1060.G365 2007
  370.15'23–dc22

18 17 16 15 14 13 12 11 10 09 08 07   1 2 3 4 5 6 7 8 9 10 11 12

• • •

*To educators, parents, and students who are
willing to learn, create, and change.*

Getting to "Got It!"

Helping Struggling Students Learn How to Learn

Acknowledgments

I am grateful for the encouragement and support of my mentors and colleagues during the research and development of these ideas. My thanks to Dr. Doris Trojcak, Dr. Louis M. Smith, Dr. Peter Wilson, Dr. Roger Clough, Dr. Tom Morgan, Dr. Sharon Lee, Dr. Kathleen Brown, Dr. Ilse Brunner, and Dr. Wayne Walker. I am also grateful to the many teachers, parents, and administrators who read drafts of the manuscript and provided valuable feedback, especially John Mackey, Kelly Powell, Ingeborg Kremshofer, Janice Duke, Cindy Buehler, Annemarie Schweiger, Sissy Mautner-Markoff, Dr. Erika Rottensteiner, Claudia Fuchs, Mary Saputo, Margaret Londal, Henrietta Baker, and critical friends in the Action Research Collaborative. Special thanks to the Danforth Foundation, the Pattonville School District, the Missouri Department of Elementary and Secondary Education, and the Missouri NEA for providing the funding that helped initiate and support the early development of this research.

I also want to thank my wonderful husband, Dr. John VanDruff, who provided love and encouragement during the writing process; my mother, Ida Kister, who instilled a love of learning very early in life; and all the students, parents, and teachers who taught me so much about how they learn. Special thanks to my editor, Katie Martin, and to ASCD for providing outstanding leadership and professional growth opportunities for educators through their publications and services.

Introduction

All teachers have seen that blank look. It's the look students give when they don't understand. We see it even after we have explained something a dozen different ways. We lose patience and ask, *Why don't they get it? It seems perfectly clear!* And when an aspect of a lesson doesn't make sense, too often the confusion and frustration students feel lead to inappropriate behaviors, and teachers get caught up trying to control or manage behaviors instead of looking at the deeper reasons why students don't understand.

While teaching art in a K–8 public school, I saw many creative, intelligent students who disliked school and became "mental dropouts." They didn't "get it," decided that they never would, and either resigned themselves to a kind of passive endurance or engaged in disruptive behaviors that drove their classroom teachers crazy and inhibited their classmates' learning. I began researching how these students could use their creativity to learn.

In my search for answers, I studied Reuven Feuerstein's (1979, 1980) work on the assessment of cognitive structures and his approach to mediated learning. In the years that followed, many other theorists and researchers—including Jean Piaget

(1950, 1954, 1969), Lev Vygotsky (2006), Jerome Bruner (2004a, 2004b), Mihalyi Csikszentmihalyi (1990, 1997), Howard Gardner (1993, 2004, 2006), Eric Jensen (2005), M. R. Jensen (2006), David Perkins (2001), Robert J. Sternberg (2003, 2004), Richard Restak (2001, 2003, 2006), David A. Sousa (2000), and L. M. Smith (1968, 1988, 2004, 2005, 2006)—influenced my ongoing efforts to help students, parents, and teachers learn more about learning.

And the students taught *me,* as well. By conducting hundreds of in-depth case studies with students who were struggling in school and then using cross-case analysis to identify patterns, I learned from the students themselves how they perceived and processed information. They taught me to see learning in a new way. I found that many students who struggled in school had underdeveloped cognitive structures, which made it difficult for them to make sense of information. Students who succeeded in school had effective cognitive structures, which made it easy to quickly process complex, abstract information.

These insights into the nature of learning have informed the approach I discuss in this book: one designed to identify and address underlying impediments to learning and help all students enhance their learning capabilities and achieve at unprecedented levels.

Cognitive Structures

Cognitive structures are basic psychological systems for gathering, organizing, and processing information. We can better understand cognitive structures by classifying them into three interdependent categories: *comparative thinking, symbolic representation,* and *logical reasoning.* In this book, I focus on the comparative thinking cognitive structures, because students use these as the foundation for developing the others.

To develop comparative thinking cognitive structures, students need to become reflectively aware of sensory input and to mentally represent (visualize) information for processing. Although cognitive structures cannot be directly taught, teachers and parents can use everyday curriculum and experiences to help students develop them. Throughout the book, I use student examples to help teachers gain insights into ways to help their students. At the end of each chapter, I offer practical suggestions to help students develop their ability to learn, create, and change.

When teachers ask me how developing cognitive structures can help struggling students overcome learning difficulties, one of the stories I like to share is Roger's.

Roger: A Creative, Frustrated Nonreader

"I can't do it!" Roger shrieked in anger and frustration as he slammed the book on the table and kicked his chair against the wall. In January, Roger's 3rd grade teacher asked me to work with Roger, who still could not read.

Reading just did not make sense to Roger, and neither the best efforts of his parents nor years of intervention from his teachers had done anything to change that. In 1st grade, Roger had been labeled learning disabled and had begun to attend daily remedial reading classes, received special education services, and participated in after-school and summer tutoring. Even with all these interventions, Roger still could not read. The words and letters he saw were disconnected bits of data that did not make sense.

Why did the dedicated efforts of Roger's teachers, tutors, and parents have so little impact? Because the efforts were all *theirs*. Learning is a creative act, and Roger, like all readers, had to *teach himself* to read. To do this, he had to develop his cognitive structures—his ability to make connections with prior knowledge and experiences, find patterns, identify predictable rules, and abstract general principles that he could apply to new and different situations.

I worked one on one with Roger for about three months in one-hour sessions twice a week. At first, he was very resistant to accepting help and tried to avoid work with his well-practiced repertoire of evasive maneuvers: dropping his pencil, falling off his chair, changing the subject, asking to go to the bathroom, and complaining that the tasks I set for him were dumb and stupid.

Each time Roger and I met, I started our interactions with nonacademic exercises that were interesting and engaging to help Roger notice patterns and relationships. I showed him how tapping into his strengths could help him develop his cognitive structures. For example, Roger was a talented artist, and when he drew pictures, he was very good at noticing details and comparing how things were alike and different. I showed him how he could use that same capability to notice details about letters and words and compare their similarities and differences. We also focused on how he could use his well-developed memory to make connections between sounds and symbols, and when he encountered something he didn't know, he could use his natural curiosity to look for patterns and relationships. Finally, we talked about how he could use his vivid imagination to visualize what words meant and make "mental videos" as he read.

By the third week of sessions, Roger was beginning to get excited about reading simple stories on his own and making sense of what he had read. We continued to start each session with puzzle-type activities specifically designed to develop his cognitive structures, and then we focused on applying these to content areas. By mid-March, Roger was reading more fluently, self-correcting his errors, and completing most assignments on his own. The boy who had screamed that he couldn't learn found that he could after all.

Cognitive Structures Develop Metability

When a person uses his or her cognitive structures, that person develops metability. I made up the word *metability*—a combination of *meta* meaning "change," as in *metamorphosis,* and *ability*—to describe the ongoing, dynamic, interactive cycle of learning, creating, and changing (see Figure 1). Learning is more than the accumulation of facts or skills. Learning is created by the learner and generates its own energy that reinforces itself through a cycle of ongoing creativity and change. Unless students interact creatively with information to construct meaning, there is little or no change. If they have not changed in some way—by gaining a new understanding, considering new ideas, acquiring additional data, or learning a new application or behavior—as a result of their interaction with information, they have not learned. The more engaged students are in creating meaning, the more they change and learn.

Figure 1	Metability as a Dynamic Cycle

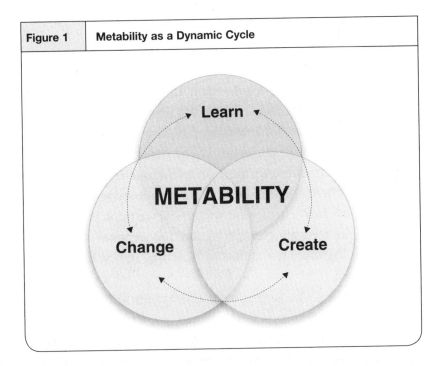

Because information in today's fast-paced, multimedia world is doubling every few months, it is crucial that our students learn how to learn—how to "figure out how to figure out"—so that they can make sense of the unfamiliar information they encounter on a daily basis. Developing cognitive structures and metability prepares students for a changing world. We don't even know all the possibilities there are around us. I like to think of a caveman sitting in a dark cave and wondering if there was a way to make light after the sun had set. In those days, that must have seemed like a crazy thought. But electricity existed, even though no one was aware of its existence. What else is "here" in our world, just waiting to be discovered and developed? With fast-paced, far-reaching developments in technology and information, our students need metability to learn, create, and change.

Learning Involves More Than Cognition

Cognitive structures and metability are permeated with what I call the "spiritual dimensions of learning," the intangible qualities that influence how students process information for understanding. These include such things as values, beliefs, feelings, assumptions, decision-making processes, expectations, attitudes, and motivations. Making meaning involves more than the brain; it also involves issues of the heart, the soul, and the spirit. The kinds of interactions and relationships we teachers have with students determine whether or not students will trust us, believe us, and accept what we offer. If we hope to reach students who are struggling, it is essential that we take into account the intangible factors that influence how they see us, themselves, and the world.

The students who step into our classrooms bring with them a wide variety of background experiences and a tremendous range of skills. We meet them where they are, and we help them move forward. My 40 years of experience as a teacher, psychological examiner, professional learning coach, university instructor, researcher, and international consultant have convinced me that helping students develop the cognitive structures they need to develop metability will help them "get it" when we teach. In this book, I provide suggestions for using this approach in daily classroom practice, advice on lesson planning for cognitive engagement, and guidelines for conducting reflective research. My hope is that you'll use what you find here not only to help struggling students break through hidden barriers to learning but to empower all students with tools that will last a lifetime.

···1···

Cognitive Structures: What They Are and Why They Matter

Imagine what it would be like to sit in a classroom and have nothing make sense. There are far too many students in our schools today who don't have to imagine this, even though today's schools are filled with dedicated teachers working hard and using research-based instructional practices in an effort to help their students learn. When we present a very well planned, logical lesson, we wonder why some students "get it" and others do not. After reexamining our methods and our curriculum, and after trying and failing again and again to reach a subset of students, we ask ourselves some hard questions: Are the students who don't get it learning disabled? Are they unmotivated? Are they unfocused, inattentive, lazy? Are they just "slow"?

To try to reach these students, our schools offer after-school study programs, remedial reading and math programs, summer school, tutoring, resource services, and special education. Still there are students who do not understand and do not achieve. Concerned parents take these students to tutors and specialists or enroll them in expensive learning centers. Still these students struggle.

Meanwhile, sitting in the same classroom with the struggling students are the high-achieving students. They thrive on our well-prepared lessons, and secretly we suspect that they could learn from anyone at any time with any kind of method. They can do this because they know how to gather, process, and output information. They have well-developed cognitive structures.

Cognitive Structures Defined

Cognitive structures are the basic mental processes people use to make sense of information. Other names for cognitive structures include *mental structures, mental tools,* and *patterns of thought.* To clarify how cognitive structures function, I group them into three interdependent categories:

1. *Comparative thinking structures* process information by identifying how bits of data are alike and different. They include *recognition, memorization, conservation of constancies, classification, spatial orientation, temporal orientation,* and *metaphorical thinking.* Comparative thinking structures are foundational to learning. As the prerequisites to the more complex cognitive structures in the other two categories, they are the focus of this book.

2. *Symbolic representation structures* transform information into culturally acceptable coding systems. They include *verbal and nonverbal language; mathematics; music and rhythms; movements, dance, and gestures; interpersonal interactions; graphics (two-dimensional drawings, paintings, logos); sculpture and constructions;* and *simulation, drama, and multimedia.*

3. *Logical reasoning structures* use abstract thinking strategies to systematically process and generate information. They include *deductive and inductive reasoning, analogical and hypothetical thinking, cause–effect relationships, analysis, synthesis, evaluation, problem framing,* and *problem solving.*

One reason that educators don't immediately identify underdeveloped or underused cognitive structures as a source of learning difficulties is that we assume they operate automatically. Our own ability to process information quickly and work easily with abstract ideas can make it difficult for us to imagine what it is like to struggle to do these things, or to grasp that it is even possible for someone over the age of 7 or 8 to *not* be able to gather and organize information, recognize patterns, or see "obvious" connections.

Often, neither the struggling students nor their teachers are aware of what lies behind the students' failure. The teachers get frustrated and conclude that the students need to pay more attention, work harder, or change their attitudes. The students have no idea why they don't get it; they think that the schoolwork is simply too hard or doesn't make sense. They may quit trying and become behavior problems, or they may slip through the cracks in the system, passing from grade to grade with minimal competency. Those who do get by typically do so by using memorization or imitation strategies. Although these tricks can help students find right answers, using them gets students no closer to experiencing the joy and excitement of deep understanding. They get no closer to developing metability.

Two Key Points

The more educators learn about how cognitive structures affect learning, the more cause there is for us to be optimistic. There are two key points to keep in mind:

1. *Each individual has to develop his or her own cognitive structures.* However, just as good coaching helps athletes improve their performance, good teaching provides learning opportunities that stimulate students' reflective awareness and visualization and help them develop their cognitive structures.

2. *It is never too late to develop cognitive structures.* From infancy through old age, everyone who has the neurological capacity to communicate, to be reflectively aware, and to use

visualization can develop cognitive structures. When I work with students who are struggling in school, I explain that they already have the capability to learn; what they need to do is learn how to use their "mental tools."

Andre: An Unmotivated 7th Grader

Andre was one of those seemingly unmotivated students who barely did enough to get by and really disliked school. I used an analogy to help him understand cognitive structures.

"Andre, do you know anyone who is really good at working on cars?" I asked.

"Yeah, my Uncle George."

"Has he got some tools he uses?"

"Oh, yeah! His garage is full of wrenches and stuff."

"He's good, right? He knows how to use his tools and make them work for him?"

"You bet!"

"If you had his tools but didn't know how to use them, would they do you any good?"

"Not really."

"What if you found out that you have mental tools in your head?"

Andre looked at me suspiciously. "What do you mean?"

"Your mind has tools, called cognitive structures, that will make learning a whole lot easier," I explained. "They'll do the work for you. Would you like that?"

"Wow!" Andre responded. "I didn't know I had tools in my head. How do I use them?"

In class, Andre normally sat back and waited for the teacher to tell him what to do. He just followed directions. When I worked with Andre, he began to use his cognitive structures to create meaning, change his understanding, and learn. He actually became excited about his "mental tools" and enjoyed the challenge of figuring things out on his own.

How Students Use Cognitive Structures to Process Information

Students use cognitive structures to process information and create meaning by (1) making connections, (2) finding patterns, (3) identifying rules, and (4) abstracting principles.

Making Connections

Cognitive structures help students make connections with prior knowledge and experience by bridging from the known to the unknown. It is very important to ask students what sense they make of information we share with them. As we listen to their connections, we show respect for their uniqueness, encourage them to bring something to the learning situation, and identify the need to clarify misconceptions.

Finding Patterns and Relationships

Cognitive structures help students compare, analyze, and organize information into patterns and relationships. Patterns are repeated motifs or units. Relationships are logical or natural associations between any two or more things. All learning is based on relationships; that is, something has meaning when compared and contrasted with something else. From early childhood, patterns are part of the curriculum. However, patterning activities remain just imitation unless the teacher uses them to mediate students' cognitive structure development. Here is an example of how Sandra came to understand patterns.

Sandra: Making Patterns

When I worked with Sandra, a 4th grader who was struggling in school, I gave her an assortment of colored paper shapes and asked her to make a pattern. She selected three big red circles and three big blue circles and then arranged them in an alternating red–blue line. She shoved all the other pieces into a pile.

When I asked Sandra to tell me about her pattern, she said, "Red–blue, red–blue, red–blue."

"What makes it a pattern?" I asked.

"The same thing goes over and over."

"What about all the other pieces?"

"They don't make a pattern."

"Help me understand," I prompted.

Sandra then became a little impatient. "That's all the big red and blue circles!"

"Are there other ways to arrange the pieces to make a pattern?" I asked.

She looked puzzled. "Huh? I don't know what you mean."

I was tempted to arrange a pattern element for her to imitate. However, for Sandra to develop her cognitive structures, she had to form patterns and relationships on her own. Too often, teachers make connections and point out patterns for students without realizing we are teaching them to imitate what we do rather than to construct meaning for themselves. Then we wonder why they cannot find patterns in reading, math, science, social studies, and life.

Sandra then asked, "What do you want me to do?"

I responded by asking her to tell me what she noticed.

"There's different colors and shapes and sizes," Sandra said.

"Tell me more," I prompted.

She started to move the pieces around and group some together. "There are big and small ones. Red, blue, yellow, green circles, squares, triangles. . . ." Sandra continued to slowly move pieces around. "Wait a minute!"

"What do you notice?" I asked.

"Wow! There are lots of different ways to make patterns!"

I watched Sandra organize a complex matrix pattern. She was smiling now. "Hey! This is fun!"

"Are there other ways you could use the pieces to make patterns?" I asked.

She paused and studied the pieces. "Let me think. Oh, yeah! Lots of ways."

"When do you see patterns in reading and writing?" I asked.

Sandra gave me a blank look and shrugged her shoulders. "I don't."

"What if you could find patterns in stories, spelling words, and sentences?"

"I don't know what you mean," Sandra replied. "Reading and spelling and stuff aren't like this. . . ."

"Everything has a pattern," I explained. "The secret to learning is finding patterns and relationships." I opened her reading book and asked what she noticed.

"What am I supposed to be looking for?" she asked. "I don't understand."

"What do you notice? See if there are patterns."

As she read, Sandra began to comment to me about how periods, commas, quotation marks, and capital letters were used. Since 1st grade, Sandra had completed many worksheets on punctuation. Now, for the first time, she noticed their patterns.

Formulating Rules

Cognitive structures help students formulate rules that make processing information automatic, fast, and predictable. When students notice relationships that are always or nearly always the same, they do not have to expend time or energy to think about them. They can divert their mental resources to new learning instead of constantly relearning the same things. Adults' definitions of rules and students' definitions often differ. Here's a conversation I had with Greg, a 5th grader.

Greg: Exploring the Meaning of Rules

I started our exploration by asking Greg, "What is a rule anyway?"

He responded, "Something you can't do."

"Give me an example," I prompted.

"Don't run in the hall. Don't fight. Don't talk out in class."

"Those are school rules. Do you have any rules at home?"

"I have to be in at a certain time," he said. "I have to clean my room."

"Do adults have rules?" I asked.

"No, they can do whatever they want. I will too, when I get big."

"Do adults have to be at work at a certain time or do what their boss tells them?"

"Well, yeah!"

"What about laws? Are laws like rules that we all have to follow?" I asked.

"Yeah."

"Where else do you have rules?"

"At restaurants you have to pay for your food and act a certain way. Don't steal."

"OK," I said, nodding. Then I prompted Greg to think beyond the negative constraints. "Have you ever thought of rules as being there to help you and keep you safe?"

"Not really."

"What about games? Could you win a game if there were no rules?"

"Sure! You can cheat!"

"How would you know if you were cheating if there were no rules? How would you know if you had any points, or won or lost?"

"Oh," he said and then paused. "I never thought of it like that."

"What if you thought about rules as being there to help you win, to make learning easier?" I suggested.

"What do you mean?"

"In math, for example, if you know the rules for multiplying and dividing, it's a lot easier to do the work," I explained. "In language arts, if you know the rules for punctuation or how to spell a word, you don't have to look it up each time." Through our interaction, Greg realized that a rule was a guide you could count on to be the same in most cases.

When working with rules, the ability to automatically predict builds confidence and enables students to quickly process more difficult and complex information. We cannot assume that *knowing a rule* is the same as *knowing when and how to use that rule*. Most teachers are trained to first teach rules and then have students apply these rules by making connections with content. I recommend instead inviting students to make connections and find patterns and relationships before asking them to formulate rules. For example, rather than teaching rules about punctuation and quotation marks, give students texts and have them work together to identify when, where, and why punctuation is used. When they identify patterns and formulate rules, they can test these rules with other texts. In addition, students are more likely to remember these rules because they created them. Does this approach take more time? Yes. Is it more effective, and will it save time in the long run? Yes.

Abstracting Generalizable Principles

Cognitive structures help students abstract generalizable principles that apply or transfer to situations other than the original learning context. Let's pause for some quick definitions. *To abstract* means to draw out or separate from a specific object or instance. A *generalizable principle* is the critical essence or fundamental guiding certainty that clarifies understanding and can be applied to diverse situations. For example, a high school sociology class studies a series of documents on social justice, and students generalize that the rights of individuals and the rights of society need to coexist in a delicate balance of power. This principle can be applied to many different historical and social settings as well as personal choices, economics, politics, literature, and the arts, just to mention a few. Many students never reach this step, because they know they can get good grades in school by just memorizing specific content. They are rarely challenged to identify generalizable principles to help them understand other information or situations in real life.

Harold: Abstracting a Principle

One afternoon I was explaining to a group of educators how students need to make connections, find patterns, formulate rules, and abstract principles. Harold, a psychologist in the group, suddenly made a connection with a childhood experience. He was 10 years old, and he and his dad were in their basement, building a birdhouse. The floor was covered with sawdust. Harold dropped a screw and immediately tried to find it by searching through all the sawdust. His dad stopped him. "Son, look where the screw fell from," he said. "Based on that, where do you think it will be?" Harold immediately looked on the floor directly below the edge of the table, reached down, and found the screw. Then his dad asked, "Will it always be that way?" This made Harold stop and think about how abstracting a generalizable principle would save time and energy.

Several things happened here. Harold's dad coached his son—in other words, he mediated meaning—by asking questions rather than telling him what to do or solving the problem for him. He not only let Harold find the screw but also taught him a valuable lesson for life. He was helping Harold develop cognitive structures by first helping him to be reflective (urging him to stop and think about an experience) and then by encouraging him to notice a relationship that was predictable. Harold's dad then went one step further to encourage him to think about abstracting a generalizable principle that would affect future experiences.

Little interactions like this have lifelong impact. Notice that Harold's father did not make fun of him, embarrass him, or call him clumsy or stupid for making a mistake. He recognized a teachable moment. We have many opportunities to coach students in such a way that helps them develop cognitive structures. As I thought about Harold's story, I realized how we often assume students are making connections, finding patterns, formulating rules, and abstracting principles, especially when things are so obvious to us. A student named Sean helped me become aware of this challenge.

Sean: A 2nd Grade Enigma

Sean's teacher described him as an enigma. He was not a behavior problem, and although he worked very hard in class, he just didn't "get it" in any content area. Sean took all his work home and brought back correctly completed worksheets. However, he could never do assignments by himself in class, nor could he explain responses on his homework papers. When I worked with Sean, he gradually began to make connections and notice patterns. Before he left, I asked him to write his name on his paper. Remembering Harold's story, I pointed to his name and asked, "Will those letters in that order always spell *Sean*?" He paused, looked at what he had written, then looked at me, and said in all sincerity, "I don't know."

I realized how critical it was for Sean to be able to generalize, so he sat back down and we worked with some math counters. We did several hands-on activities, such as moving a set of five blocks around to see how many different ways he could make them equal 5. As Sean made each arrangement of blocks, I asked rule-oriented questions. For example, "Would 1 + 4 *always* equal 5?" He would have to check it out several times before being certain that 1 + 4 and 4 + 1, or 2 + 3 and 3 + 2, would *always* equal 5. We did this with several different numbers.

Then I had Sean write the words *rat* and *tar*.

I asked, "What do you notice about these words?"

Sean said, pointing to *rat* and *tar,* "These two have the same letters, but they're lined up different."

"Will *r-a-t* always spell *rat*?" I asked him.

Sean thought for a few minutes. Then he looked at me and responded cautiously, "Yes, I think so."

"Will *t-a-r* always spell *tar*?"

Sean responded a little more confidently, "Yes."

I then asked him what had changed and what had stayed the same. He pointed out that the letters had stayed the same but that the order and meaning had changed. After practicing with several words, Sean looked up at me and said confidently, "I get it! Some things are the same even when some things change!"

Sean's teacher noticed an immediate change in his participation and productivity in class. A couple weeks later, I went to Sean's classroom to check on him. Students were quietly doing a spelling worksheet. When Sean saw me at the door, he smiled and motioned for me to come over to his desk. As I looked to see what he was doing, he pointed to a word on his paper. He said, "That's *cake,* and it will always spell *cake*!" I was as happy as he was. Sean was a young man who worked very hard with little or no understanding or enjoyment in learning until he figured out that simple principle: *Some things change; some things stay the same.* Before he learned to generalize, every piece of information was new and different, and he felt completely overwhelmed. Now he was looking for connections, patterns, rules, and generalizable principles that would make it easier for him to learn.

Three Important Questions About Cognitive Structures

When educators begin to understand what cognitive structures are and how they work, they ask three important questions.

1. How do students develop cognitive structures?

2. Why have some students already developed them and other students have not?

3. What can a teacher do to help students develop cognitive structures?

How Do Students Develop Cognitive Structures?

Students develop cognitive structures through *reflective awareness* and through *visualization*. The more students become reflectively aware of what their senses are telling them and mentally represent this information through visualization, the stronger their cognitive structures will become and the more likely they will be to develop metability to learn, create, and change (see Figure 1.1).

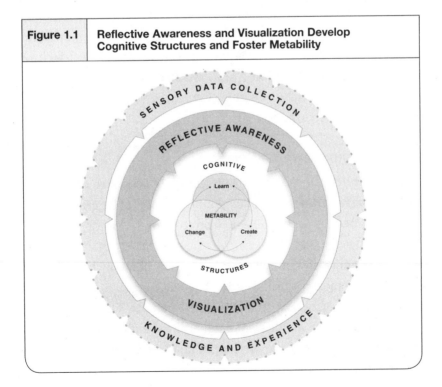

| Figure 1.1 | Reflective Awareness and Visualization Develop Cognitive Structures and Foster Metability |

Reflective awareness. Reflective awareness is conscious perception. *Reflection* is thoughtful consideration. *Awareness* is alert attention. To be *conscious* means to be mindfully attentive of oneself as a thinking, feeling person. To *perceive* means to mentally take hold of or consciously grasp something while assigning meaning to it. The mind accepts mental representations of information as fact. Perception is reality for the person doing the perceiving. Perception is filtered through values, beliefs, and feelings, which color and shape how the information is processed. Perception can be intuitive and unsystematic, or it can be reflective and logical. Although reflective awareness is similar to metacognition, it is, more simply, thinking about your thinking.

Students take in sensory data every waking minute. To be reflectively aware, students need to notice and thoughtfully consider the information that they see, hear, touch, taste, and smell. We have all had students with learning problems and ones who have demonstrated inappropriate behavior, a disrespectful attitude, poor cooperation, a lack of productivity, or a lack of motivation. When I work with students like these, I focus on helping them develop more effective cognitive structures. Here is the story of one such student.

Tim: An Unproductive 8th Grader

Tim slouched in a chair across from me, gazing into space as if he were bored to death. I placed an open box of 24 crayons and a pile of 5 pencils on the desk in front of him. "What do you see?" I asked.

Tim glanced at the materials. "A bunch of stuff," he replied.

"Tell me more," I prompted.

"It's just a bunch of stuff—crayons, pencils. That's all."

Once we make a judgment such as "that's all," we cut off sensory input, and with little sensory data, there is little information to process. My objective was to help Tim become reflectively aware of the millions of bits of sensory data available to him.

"What do you notice?" I asked, gesturing to crayons and pencils on the table.

"Huh? What do you mean?" he asked me.

Tim was waiting for me to tell him what I wanted for a response, to tell him what he *should* see and notice. Too often, well-meaning parents and teachers short-circuit students' cognitive development by doing the mental work for them. For example, we give them some objects to sort and tell them how to sort those objects rather than giving them the objects and letting them figure out several possible criteria for sorting. We unintentionally encourage them to become passive recipients, to depend on others rather than on their own capabilities or need to know.

"Trust your eyes and your brain," I told Tim. "What do you notice?"

"Well, OK, I notice the box is open," Tim said. "And inside there's lots of different colors. Some are just different shades of the same color. Like here." He sat up in the chair and reached out to slide the crayons out of the box onto the desk. "There's light green, regular green, kelly green," Tim said, reading the labels on the crayons. "There's blue-green and turquoise."

"Tell me more," I said.

Tim started feeling the crayons and pencils, gathering tactile data. "They're round, or really kinda shaped like. . . ." He paused. "I forget what you call that shape."

"Cylinder shape," I said.

"Yeah, cylinder, that's it. And they're made of wax. When I was a kid, I used to like to color," Tim said. He smiled as he cocked his head to one side and pretended to be coloring a picture. "These pencils are made of wood and have a little rubber on the end with metal around to hold it on. I like to draw, too."

"I bet you are good at drawing," I commented.

"Yeah," Tim said. "It's fun, you know? I look at something and then draw it on the paper. I make up stuff to draw too, like from my mind."

"Have you ever thought of using your imagination to learn?" I asked.

"Huh?"

"I bet that before you draw something, you can actually see it in your mind, right?"

"Yeah. I know exactly what it's going to look like."

"You think about it, too, right?" I asked. "You see in your mind how all the parts fit together?"

Tim smiled and nodded. "Yeah," he replied.

"What if you found out that you could use that same ability to reflect and picture things in your mind to learn stuff in school?"

"That would be pretty cool."

Teachers often form an unspoken agreement with unproductive students like Tim. It goes something like this: "You don't bother me, and I won't bother you." These students drift through their schooling, putting in time, staying out of trouble, and doing just enough work to squeak by. Tim knew he wasn't dumb because he could figure out what to do in many different kinds of real-life situations. But he had decided, back when he was in elementary school, that the "school stuff" was hard, no fun, and not worth his time and energy. The way to reach these students is to encourage them to notice data available to their senses. The process of reflective awareness helps students develop their cognitive structures to process information and create meaning. If students fail to notice what their senses are telling them or fail to reflect on the information they take in, they quickly discard it, unprocessed.

Students who demonstrate ADD or ADHD behaviors use a kind of blurred and sweeping perception that limits sensory input. This kind of superficial information gathering is reinforced by the value that our fast-paced society places on speed. Movies, TV shows, commercials, and video games with rapidly flashing images and sounds foster lack of attention. Noise and commotion overload senses without processing. Students are often hurried from one activity to another with little time for reflection. Without sufficient data and reflection, students have difficulty determining what is relevant.

Visualization. As students become reflectively aware of the messages or stimulation their senses are sending to their brains, they need to visualize the information so that they can process it. Visualization is the ability to mentally represent and manipulate information, ideas, feelings, and sensory experiences. It is essential in abstract thinking and planning. Without visualization, students are dependent on specific information within sensory range and have a very difficult time with abstract thinking.

When we visualize, we use images, symbols (e.g., numbers, words, pictures, designs, and diagrams), and other forms of mental coding to represent sounds, tastes, smells, feelings, experiences, and information. These mental representations are so real that the mind often cannot differentiate between what is outside (in the material world) and what is inside (in the mind).

Imagination is important, but being able to differentiate what is real and what is imaginary is important too. This is especially true when students get so engrossed in virtual characters—TV, movie, or video game superheroes, for example—that they walk around acting like and thinking they are the character, even trying to do super-karate maneuvers or gravity-defying tricks they have observed.

Jerry: In Trouble on the Bus

Jerry, a 2nd grader, was constantly getting in trouble on the bus. No amount of behavior modification seemed to change his bizarre reactions to other students and his apparently uncontrollable jumping around and yelling. Although Jerry was doing well academically, his teacher was very concerned about his inappropriate behavior on the bus because it was resulting in suspensions and missed classes.

Using reflective awareness and visualization, Jerry was able to identify the causes of his behavior. He described how the other kids made him feel and act like the title character from TV's *Buffy the Vampire Slayer.* When I asked him to help me understand, Jerry said, "Well, I'm like Buffy: fighting and overcoming evil forces. When the other kids say something mean, I jump over the seat and try to knock them out, or I crawl under the seats to escape." In a matter-of-fact way, he demonstrated how he swung his imaginary sword to take on his foes. I asked Jerry if he really thought the other kids were vampires or other evil monsters, and he replied confidently, "That's what they look like to me!"

Together Jerry and I did some sensory input exercises and some visualization exercises to help him differentiate between what his senses were seeing and hearing, and what his mind was making up. I also worked with him to identify alternative behaviors he could use to deal with the situation. One of the exercises took advantage of his very active imagination: practicing thinking "beautiful thoughts" that made him feel calm and happy inside. "Picture something that makes you feel so good that you don't want to quit thinking about it," I advised. He liked that idea. He was soon able to ride the bus without further incident.

A couple weeks later, I saw Jerry on the playground and asked if he was still thinking beautiful thoughts. He said smilingly, "Oh, I don't have to think them anymore. They just come all by themselves!" In general, I've found the "beautiful thought" exercise to be a marvelous way to help students settle themselves and encourage both reflective awareness and visualization.

Here's an example of how John's teacher helped him discover that his ability to visualize could make his schoolwork more enjoyable.

John: Using His "Mental Hands"

John was an 8th grader who hated school and did just barely enough work to pass each year. Although he was not a behavior problem, his teachers and parents became frustrated because he refused to do his work. However, John loved to draw and often amazed the other kids with his exceptional drawing abilities. One day his teacher took some time to work one on one with John to find how he could use his strengths to be successful in school.

John's teacher used an assessment instrument called the tower, which is designed to identify and develop a student's cognitive structures. The instrument consists of six small boards, five by five centimeters square and about one and a half centimeters thick. The boards are painted black, and each is drilled with nine evenly spaced holes. Each hole is fitted with a black peg, about two centimeters high, and on each of the boards, one of the pegs is glued into its hole. The six boards with their pegs are stacked to form a tower (see Figure 1.2). The positions of the glued pegs all together form an asymmetrical pattern.

Figure 1.2	The Tower: An Instrument for Cognitve Structure Assessment and Development

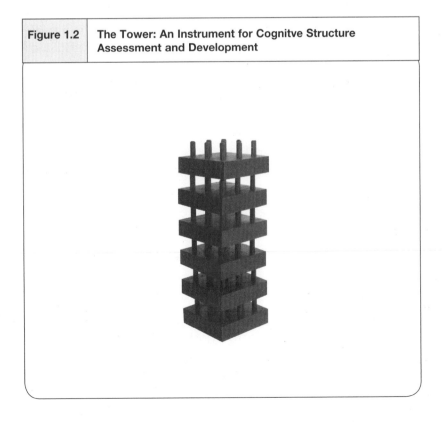

When John and his teacher started working together, the teacher asked him to describe what he saw (what his senses were telling him). Instead of saying that he saw six black blocks stacked on each other, John said that he saw a parking garage, a building under construction, and a jail. He never mentioned the color, shape, size, position, or other sensory data. Like so many creative students, John immediately visualized, processed, and interpreted his perception instead of the information itself. This is a real gift for creative expression; however, when it comes to schoolwork it can be a problem because the information processed is not what is required for assignments and tests. This is one reason so many creative students have problems in school. John's teacher explained that he was "seeing with his mind," which was a wonderful ability to have, but that it was important for him to also see with his eyes and notice what his eyes were telling his brain. John then described the visual characteristics of the tower.

Next, his teacher asked him to twist the pegs on each board to find the glued peg. As he found each one, he identified its location in relationship to the other pegs; for example, "On Block 1, the glued peg is in the middle left." Identifying the position was easy for John; however, if students do not effectively use spatial cognitive structures, they have a difficult time naming the position. As he found each glued peg, he removed the block from the stack and set it on the table. Every time he found a glued peg, John closed his eyes and made a mental map; that is, he visualized glued positions in relationship to each other. He repeated unstacking the tower several times until he was confident that he could visualize the pattern. To confirm that John had visualized the information and to have him symbolically represent it, his teacher drew a tic-tac-toe grid on a piece of paper and asked John to write the numbers 1 to 6 on the grid to show where the pegs were glued. Without hesitation, John identified the positions (see Figure 1.3). "I can see it," he said, pointing to his head.

His teacher removed the paper, stacked the blocks, and rotated the tower clockwise one quarter-turn. Then the teacher said, "Use

Figure 1.3	John's Mental Map of the Tower

4		6
1		5
	3	2

your mental map and pick up each block by the glued peg." John smiled and quickly unstacked the blocks without error.

"How did you do that so quickly?" his teacher asked.

John said, "Well, I just took my mental hands and turned it around in my head."

"Mental hands? Tell me about your mental hands," his teacher prompted.

John responded, "Well, when I want to draw something, I take my mental hands and turn it around in my head. Then I can see it from all sides, and I can draw anything."

With enthusiasm, the teacher followed up and asked John if he'd ever thought of using his mental hands to do math, language, science, or history. John said no and then asked how he could do that. His teacher suggested visualizing what the numbers stand for in math or what the story is saying in history.

John was a bit surprised that he could use what he was good at—his mental hands—to do schoolwork. Within three months, he went from the bottom of his class to the 8th grade honor roll. An even more important accomplishment was that John continued to use his mental hands over the next four years and graduated from high school in the top 10 percent of his class. Learning to use his own visualization ability made school much more meaningful and enjoyable for John. He no longer had to avoid schoolwork because now he could make sense of it.

Why Have Some Students Developed Cognitive Structures and Others Have Not?

As noted, students develop cognitive structures by being reflectively aware of sensory input and by visualizing information for processing. It's often the case that many so-called "smart" students are those who have received the most effective mediation at home. Encouraged to visualize and reflect from an early age, they come to school with well-developed cognitive structures. Students who appear "slow" due to underdeveloped cognitive structures may have grown up with little mediation or encouragement for reflection and visualization. Other circumstances that can inhibit cognitive structure development include

- Physical impairments or psychological disorders
- Living in poverty with limited access to resources
- Trauma or abuse
- Fragmented family structures, isolation, or insecurity
- Limited verbal interaction or communication difficulties attributable to language barriers
- Extended illness
- A home life in which learning is devalued

Although these circumstances are outside educators' control, we can accept students and believe it is possible for them to develop their cognitive structures.

What Can a Teacher Do to Help Students Develop Their Cognitive Structures?

Because students have to develop their own expertise in using cognitive structures, teachers can help by encouraging them to develop the following skills:

- Become reflectively aware of sensory data

- Visualize information
- Ask questions and conduct experiments to figure things out on their own

For students to believe and trust us, we teachers must have a caring relationship with them. We also need to ask stimulating questions and provide opportunities for them to make mistakes in safe environments where they don't need to worry about "feeling stupid."

We can use everyday lessons, activities, and content to help students develop cognitive structures (see Figure 1.4). Although we work within a set curriculum, this goal can influence our choices about what and how we teach. If, for example, our goal is simply raising test scores, we will only teach what is tested. If our goal is developing metability, we will use lessons designed to develop the cognitive structures that equip students to learn, create, and change.

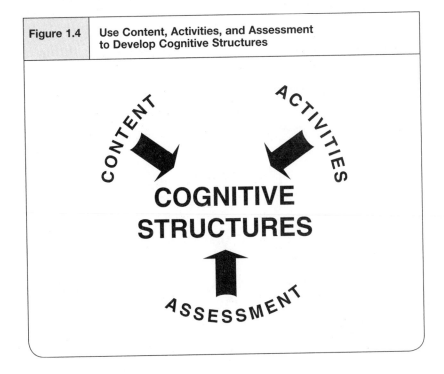

| Figure 1.4 | Use Content, Activities, and Assessment to Develop Cognitive Structures |

As teachers begin to understand how students need to use cognitive structures to make sense of information presented in class, they analyze their lessons in terms of these two questions: (1) Which cognitive structures are needed for this content, activity, and assessment? (2) How can I use the content, activity, and assessment to help students develop these cognitive structures?

Teachers often complain they don't have time to cover all the required content, and they are right. I worked with a history teacher who was expected to cover everything from the European Middle Ages through the Renaissance in six weeks. She said, "I feel like I'm flying an airplane but nobody's on it!" Similar situations exist in other content areas. Because students are exposed to new concepts almost every day without time for processing, they memorize as much as they can and usually forget it within a week or two.

Sometimes teachers get caught up in doing lots of activities that keep students busy and may even produce wonderful products or displays. However, the time would be more effectively spent designing and implementing activities to help students develop the cognitive structures that will equip them for independent learning. For example, Tami, a 5th grade teacher, came to one of the group meetings after doing a science lesson on bubbles. She was exhausted, frustrated, and disgusted.

Tami's Bubble Lesson for 5th Graders

"I'm never doing bubbles again!" Tami complained at our meeting. "My kids made such a mess, just goofed off, started squirting soap and chasing each other around. It was awful!"

"Did you ask them what they noticed about bubbles?" I asked. "Or what they learned from doing the activity?"

"No. I forgot to do that," Tami said. "I just followed the plan in the book."

Tami told me that although she usually enjoyed doing fun activities with her students, she was sometimes disappointed when students seemed to miss the point of the activity. Although Tami was an experienced teacher, she had the courage to admit that it was difficult for her to make the connection between activities and cognitive structures. She began to seriously analyze how she could plan activities to help the students develop and use their cognitive structures.

Through discussion with colleagues in the seminar, she realized that she could have interacted with the group and with individuals as they were experimenting with the bubbles and stimulated reflective awareness by asking questions. For example, she could have asked: "What do you notice?" "Why do you think this is happening?" "What if . . . ?" "What do you understand about bubbles?" "What questions come to mind?" "What do you wonder about?" "Why do you need to know this?" "What does this have to do with life?"

After the discussion, Tami asked her students these questions and requested that they submit responses in writing. At first, her students moaned and groaned, because they just wanted to do another fun activity. However, Tami encouraged them to reflect on what they had learned from the bubble activity. As the students began to share their "notices," questions, and what they wondered about, Tami suddenly realized that every activity could be an opportunity for her students to use and develop their cognitive structures. With this activity, her role was to help them do the following:

- Notice what changed and what stayed the same (conservation of constancy).
- Compare and contrast attributes (classification).
- Notice where and when bubbles formed and floated (time and space).
- Find ways to describe and document observations and experiences (symbolic representation).
- Analyze cause–effect relationships (logical thinking).
- Make creative comparisons (metaphorical thinking).

By using their cognitive structures to process the information and components of the activity, Tami's students were developing their metability.

It took time for Tami to become comfortable with this approach. Several weeks later she came to the group meeting and confessed that she was feeling a little guilty. "I'm not up there doing my 'teacher thing' anymore," she said. "Now, I get the kids started, they begin asking questions, and then they do their work. I go around and help as needed, but they're so involved, it's like they're teaching themselves. I can't believe how relaxing it is!"

Traditionally, we use standardized, formal, and informal testing to assess learning. Students may come to think the grade is more important than understanding. Sometimes teachers give students study guides to memorize for a test. However, if the questions are rephrased on the test, students are lost.

Assessments encourage effective use of cognitive structures when students integrate and apply information. We can assess understanding by encouraging students to formulate questions (not ones they can copy an answer to from the text). *The true level of understanding is evident in the kinds of questions students ask.* Teachers who model asking open-ended questions stimulate student reflection and the need to know more. We can also encourage students to assess their own understanding by asking them to explain information to a younger student.

We are trained in content, methods, and assessment. We are under immense pressure to cover material and raise test scores. We have limited resources and time for instruction, and we still must deal with other issues, such as schedules, discipline, classroom management, administrative paperwork, special needs students, and so on. Therefore it is more efficient (not more effective) to simply give the students a worksheet and have them fill in the correct responses. Some teachers will object and say, "I don't do that!" Interestingly, it is challenging for most teachers to step back and analyze their beliefs and practices about teaching and learning. As I work with teacher groups, I encourage them to videotape their lessons and bring the tapes to the group for analysis. It is truly a "eureka" moment when they realize they do most of the talking (even answering their own questions) and encourage imitation rather than cognitive processing. They also notice how they assume everyone in class understands when one student responds correctly, and how they (not the students) are doing most of the work. Through discussion, the teachers also begin to see how their curriculum can help develop the cognitive structures needed for metability.

Although I see that it is challenging for these teachers to transform their thinking and embrace this new focus, they always express relief and renewed energy when they see their students learn, create, and change. One teacher with 28 years of experience commented, "Why weren't we taught this in our teacher training? How did I ever get through all these years not knowing this? This is so much more enjoyable and satisfying for me and the kids!"

Suggestions for Practice

1. *Build caring relationships with your students.* They will believe you and work with you if they trust you and know you care for them. Spend time with them. Listen to them.

2. *Encourage students to be reflectively aware.* Prompt them to notice what their senses are telling them. Allow time for them to wonder about their thoughts and reactions. Encourage them to suspend judgment and delay output to allow for effective processing of information.

3. *Encourage students to use their imaginations to visualize.* When students can picture (or hear, feel, taste, or smell) data in their minds, they can carry it with them when the information is

out of sensory range. Visualizing helps transform physical data into abstract representations.

4. *Encourage students to use cognitive structures to process information* in the following ways:

- Make connections with prior knowledge and experience and share what they bring to the learning situation. Ask them to explain how they put things together in their mind and why they do it the way they do.
- Look for patterns and relationships among bits of information to integrate and make meaning. Ask students how they can move the bits of data around to make different kinds of patterns.
- Formulate rules to process information quickly and automatically. Rules are guidelines or predictable patterns that provide structure. Applying rules in appropriate situations uses less mental energy than constantly relearning information or ways of doing things.
- Abstract generalizable principles to transfer learning from one situation to another.

5. *Mediate meaning for students.* Model, coach, question, listen to, and encourage students. Analyze content, activities, and assessments to identify which cognitive structures are needed for the lesson and how to use the lesson to develop cognitive structures.

6. *Encourage students to ask questions and to wonder.* This is especially important to clarify their interpretations of what they see, hear, and experience so they don't form misconceptions. Encourage students to ask themselves: "What does this mean to me?" and "How would I explain this to someone in my own words?" When students begin to ask themselves these questions, they become their own teachers.

7. *Instead of "telling," use open-ended prompts and questions.*

Here are some examples:

- What sense do you make of this?
- What questions come to mind as you think about this?
- Which part do you know for sure? Which part do you understand?
- What do you notice?
- What kind of pattern do you notice?
- What do you wish was easier? (Students will respond to let you know where they need help.)
- Why? (Ask this question to encourage students to elaborate on their responses—without giving them nonverbal clues about whether their responses are correct.)
- What did you understand the question to be?
- What do you wonder about?
- How is this like life?
- If you were going to explain this to someone, how would you do it?
- If you did know, what would you say? (Use this when students respond to a question by shrugging their shoulders or saying, "I don't know.")
- Tell me in your own words what you understand.
- Tell me more.
- Help me understand.

... 2 ...

Recognition

It was a frosty Thanksgiving morning when I drove up to my sister's farmhouse in a remote rural area where the family gathered for the holiday. From the backseat, my 2-year-old son, Paul, said, "We were here last year at this house. I remember the barn." This was just one of many occasions when Paul amazed me by recognizing things that he had seen and heard before.

Students begin learning by building a database of sensory input, and then recognizing that they have previously seen it, heard it, tasted it, touched it, smelled it, or otherwise "sensed" it. For example, a newborn baby compares a face it sees to Mama's face, the sound of a voice to Papa's voice, and so on with taste, touch, and smell. Something as simple as recognition is a very complex mental operation. Because recognition happens in a split second, it is challenging to slow down the process to understand how it works.

Recognition Defined

Recognition is the ability to identify a match or fit between two or more pieces of information. It is one of the first cognitive structures we learn to use—and one that we often take for granted.

Here is an example of recognition. A small child sees a dog for the first time, hears it barking, and then touches, smells, or even tries to taste it. Initial sensory input provides isolated bits of data. When the child sees or hears a dog again, he mentally represents and processes the data by comparing the two samples (recognizing, recalling, and classifying). It takes several encounters like this for the child to recognize characteristics of "dog-ness" that apply to many different kinds of dogs. Gradually, he begins to associate specific combinations of sounds (words) as names for the information. Using words or images, the child can mentally represent *dog* even when no dog is present.

As students grow and learn, they continue to expand their experiential database. The more experiences they have, the more likely they are to have a fit when they compare new experiences with previous ones. It is fascinating to watch very young children recognize things they have seen or heard before. Recognizing patterns enables us to process information more quickly. Recognition of the familiar builds confidence and a feeling of security; it helps students feel confident enough to reach out to what is unfamiliar. It also triggers emotions and memories.

Sometimes students confuse recognition with knowing. For example, they may be studying for a test in science and flip through the pages of the text, saying to themselves, "Yeah, yeah, yeah, I know this." What they really mean is, "I recognize this information. I have seen it or heard it before." When they must respond to questions designed to test their understanding of the information, these students struggle. Multiple-choice test questions often assess recognition more than understanding.

As adults, we continue to use and develop recognition each time we encounter new information. When we travel to a foreign country, for example, we instinctively look for things we recognize to help us adjust to our new surroundings. If we go to the supermarket and see a fruit or vegetable we have never seen before, we might touch it, smell it, or even request a taste. We compare the data we collect with other things that we know to see if we can recognize something familiar: Does the unfamiliar fruit have a rind like citrus? Is its texture crisp, like an apple? Is it sour, like a lemon, or sweet, like a peach?

In many professions, proficient recognition of visual patterns is essential. For example, fighter pilots have to recognize visual data in a split second, and physicians have to recognize symptoms for diagnosis. Musicians recognize melodic motifs and rhythms; writers and artists recognize styles and themes; and professional athletes and dancers recognize patterns of movements. And today's computer technology amplifies and speeds up the process of recognition by using sophisticated systems of comparison to identify fit. Because information and technology are changing so rapidly, we need to help students learn to use cognitive structures effectively to enhance metability—the ability to learn, create, and change.

Helping Students Develop Recognition

Educators cannot develop students' cognitive structures; students have to do it on their own. What we can do is enhance their ability to gather and process information by encouraging them to notice and visualize what their senses are telling them. Just looking at something or hearing sounds, such as verbal directions, does not guarantee input or processing. Sometimes we are tempted to tell students what to recognize or notice, and then we assume that because we told them, they have learned it. The most effective way to mediate is to be attentive, listen, and ask students to help us understand how they make connections in their own minds. We can ask the following types of questions: What do you see (or hear, feel, smell, taste)? What does that remind you of? What do you notice? How would you describe this to someone who is not here? Young students are usually full of questions. If they feel safe, without fear of being made fun of or feeling stupid, they will continue to ask questions. After answering questions and explaining things to students, ask them to describe in their own words what they understood from what they heard.

For students to read and write, they need to recognize that they have seen or heard a letter, sound, or word before. If they have not developed effective recognition, every time they see or hear a letter, sound, or word, it is as if they are encountering it for the first time. They cannot recognize having seen it before unless they are reflectively aware when they look at it the first time.

Pat Sees "Pat" in "Pattern"

Pat, a 2nd grader, couldn't read. The first couple of times I worked with him, he was very engaged in the activities and became more reflectively aware of what his senses were telling him. After our third session, he returned to his classroom in the middle of math lesson. When he saw the worksheet on his desk, he went up to his teacher, pointed to the word *pattern* on the sheet, and said, "My name is in that word."

His teacher, who had training in cognitive structures, became very excited. She knew that Pat's ability to compare and recognize a word pattern was the first step to reading. Within a week, Pat started to read. During our next session, he read Dr. Seuss's *The Cat in the Hat* all the way through. He asked if he could borrow the book. He returned to his class and asked his teacher if he could read it to the class. She was so happy that she stopped the lesson and they all celebrated as Pat read his first book out loud to the class. The teacher could not wait to tell me about the "breakthrough!"

Suggestions for Practice

1. *Encourage students to consciously focus and notice what they see* (and hear, touch, taste, and smell). Students can learn

to gather relevant sensory data by noticing details such as color, shape, size, position, texture, and relationships. The more information they gather, the more data they have for comparison and recognition. Listen when students say they recognize something; this provides valuable insight into how to mediate meaning for them.

2. *Encourage students to compare new information with what they have seen and heard before.* Instead of continually presenting new information, give the students the opportunity to think about how one bit of information is alike and different from other things that they have seen, heard, or experienced. Encourage them to recognize different characteristics (beyond the obvious) that stimulate their creativity.

3. *Encourage students to reflect and visualize* what they see, hear, and experience to allow time for recognition and processing. Visualization facilitates mental manipulation of information when input is out of sensory range.

4. *Remember that recognition of the familiar makes students feel more confident.* It enables students to predict what is to come and to deal with the unfamiliar. Provide opportunities for students to enjoy experiencing the same thing over and over (for example, familiar tunes, videos, stories, sights, and sounds).

5. *Encourage students to look at text and identify words that they recognize.* There are many simple games and toys to help students develop recognition. These include matching games with letters, words, numbers, shapes, colors, and patterns; face, voice, and sound recognition games; scavenger hunts; Bingo; and puzzles.

···3···

Memorization

"Seven, 14, 21, 28, 35, 42, 49, 56, 63, 70, 77, 84."

Allen, a 4th grader, proudly rattled off his seven times tables for me. He was just about to start in on "his eights" when I stopped him and asked him what those numbers meant.

"Huh?" he responded. "What do you mean? It's the times tables."

"I know. And it's very important to know them. Why did you learn them?" I asked.

"'Cause I had to. And there was a prize for knowing them. My mama worked with me to learn them."

When I prompted Allen again to tell me what the times tables meant, he was confused. "Mean? They're just numbers. I have a test on them too."

Like many students, Allen memorized times tables without understanding what they are, why he needed to know them, or how to use them. Allen learned early that getting right answers was more important than understanding. He also worked very hard each week to memorize his spelling words and always got 100 percent; however, he could rarely define them or spell them correctly when writing. Allen was simply mimicking or imitating the patterns of numbers or words. Imitation is a preliminary form of memorization. From infancy through adulthood, we learn by imitating. For example, to learn a skill, we imitate others who have mastered it. Imitation becomes a limitation when we *only* do what others do. Students sometimes confuse imitation with learning. In the classroom, they may correctly complete assignments by simply imitating what the teacher models, without making the information their own. They often have difficulty working independently without a model in front of them. For students to learn, create, and change, they need to use their cognitive structures to process the information instead of just imitating what is presented.

Memorization Defined

Memorization is a cognitive structure for storing and recalling information. The more connections we make through recognition and classification, the more likely we are to remember information. Although teachers have different points of view about memorization, they agree that students need to remember what is taught. It is impossible to function in this world without some form of memorization.

Contrary to popular belief, memory is not a mental file cabinet where we simply store facts and knowledge and pull them back out again as needed. Although rote memory stores bits of data without integration with existing knowledge, memorization as a cognitive structure activates different parts of the mind to reconstruct information. To help students understand this, I compare learning to the process of digesting food. I explain that what we know and remember has to be processed to become a part of us on a mental level, just as the food we eat doesn't stay whole but is transformed through digestion, absorption, and metabolism into small molecules that are then reassembled to construct cells of our body.

There is a difference between understanding and memorizing. For example, we can understand what we read or see, but to remember it, we have to consciously process it for access. In school, students often experience an overload of new information, along with the need to recall on demand. Without the opportunity or ability to effectively process information, they question why they need to know it, or they resort to memorization, guessing, or mental disengagement.

The cognitive structure of memorization includes what is usually described as three types, or *stages,* of memory:

- *Short-term memory* temporarily remembers information available to the senses.
- *Continuous memory* makes connections with prior knowledge and experiences.
- *Long-term memory* makes information accessible depending on how effectively it is processed.

Continuous memory and long-term memory involve physical and mental skills that become automatic with practice and easily accessible when the person has a repertoire of processed information. Although the three types of memory appear to work in a linear or sequential manner, they function in a cyclical, interactive manner and process information on multiple levels simultaneously. Integrated information is more likely to be remembered and accessible than disconnected bits of data. Research is showing that several different parts of the brain are activated to reconstruct memories. Memorized information is *procedural,* dealing with the way things are done, or *declarative,* recording data and events along with their personal meaning.

Memory strategies, which are methods of making connections to aid memory, include mnemonics, acrostics, chunking, rhymes, rhythms, concept mapping, outlining, sequences, cartooning, applications, and contextual references. Multisensory input, visualization, and application of information enhance the effectiveness of these strategies.

Many factors affect how data is processed for memorization, including the following:

- *Emotions* associated with information or events as well as one's emotional state at the time.
- *Purpose* or reason to remember something based on relevance or need.
- *Beliefs and values,* which filter or evaluate information based on perceived level of credibility or importance.
- *Kind and quality of information gathered,* which determine how accurate and usable the information is.
- *Prior knowledge and experience,* including level of expertise.

Helping Students Develop Memory

Teachers can mediate students' memory development by encouraging them to visualize and be reflectively aware of how they make connections, identify patterns, formulate rules, and abstract principles to create meaning. They might do this by classifying information for access, contextualizing it in time and space, labeling it with words or other symbols, and identifying specific logical or metaphorical connections. Consider also that memory is enhanced with positive or negative emotional associations; the stronger the emotional bond, the more vivid the memory. Although some students remember more by hearing and others, by seeing, most remember by doing because action involves multiple sensory inputs.

Memorized information that is integrated with meaning builds confidence and self-esteem because it helps students know what they know for sure and provides a database for new connections. Sometimes memories change over time because they are compared to other events or perspectives; in other words, new events, feelings, or information color or influence the original data.

At a very early age, students learn that those who remember what is presented in class are considered smart and those who forget are considered dumb. They begin to feel that something is wrong with them if they can't remember things.

"Can't-Remember" Candace

By 3rd grade, Candace was convinced she was not good at remembering. Her parents were constantly after her for forgetting. Her teacher was concerned that she might have attention deficit disorder because she could not remember simple procedures such as turning in her homework, following directions, and using what she learned from one day to the next.

When Candace first came to see me in October, she introduced herself: "I'm Can't-Remember Candace." She was nervous and self-conscious, looking around and twisting her hands together as she slid into a chair. She told me that all her life (she was 8 years old), she'd forgotten things. "Everyone says I can't remember," Candace said. "I'm no good at it."

"Would you like to be able to remember?" I asked.

Her response was, "I can't."

What Candace had heard others say about her she was now saying to herself. I saw that my first task was to help her see that she could build expertise with the cognitive structure of memorization. When I asked her to spell her name, and she did, I pointed out that she remembered that.

"That's easy. That's not like remembering school stuff and how to do things."

"Let's see what you can do. It is 1:15 and you will be here until 2:15," I said. Candace looked at the clock. "Can you tell time?" I asked.

"Yes," she responded.

"You remembered how to do that, right?"

"Yeah, because there are clocks everywhere. That's easy."

Without realizing it, Candace was demonstrating that she *was* capable of remembering information. I continued to do some simple nonacademic activities with her. For example, I gave her a design, made of geometric shapes and asked her to draw it. She looked at it and quickly drew it. I asked her what she noticed about the design, and she described details: one square was bigger than the other and the squares overlapped. To identify these details, she was using the cognitive structures of recognition, spatial orientation, conservation of constancy, classification, and verbal tools. I put her drawing in a folder. By this time, Candace was relaxed. I asked her to tell me more about incidents when she wished she could remember things.

"Like when the teacher tells me what to do. I can't remember what she said."

"OK, how does that make you feel?"

"I get all scared that I'm going to get it all wrong. I used to ask her to tell me again, but she always tells me to pay attention, so I just look around and copy what everybody's doing."

"What about your homework?" I asked.

"I can't remember what to do or how to do it. I forget everything!"

"Do you get on the right bus to go home? And get off at the right stop?"

Candace responded, "Yes, it's right by where I live."

"You remember where you live?"

"Yes." She looked at me as if I were silly for asking such a question.

"How do you remember that?" I asked.

"Because that's where I live!"

"Well, it looks to me like you can remember lots of things," I pointed out to her.

Candace sat back, cocked her head to one side, and paused to think. We continued to talk about things that she did remember.

I then gave her a blank paper and asked her to draw the design she had drawn before. At first, she gasped in panic at the thought of having to remember something she did "such a long time ago." She hesitated to even pick up the pencil. She just sat there shaking her head no.

"I can't!" Candace said.

"Wait a minute. Close your eyes and see in your mind the different shapes you drew on the paper. Let your mind do the work for you," I prompted.

She closed her eyes for a few seconds and then slowly picked up her pencil and began to draw. Candace paused a couple of times, closed her eyes to think, and then continued. When she had finished, I opened the folder and showed her the original. She was surprised to see that she had remembered all but one small circle. Candace demonstrated to herself that she had the capability of visualizing and remembering images. She had never thought of using her imagination to help her remember. When I asked her if she remembered what time we started and when we were going to stop, she looked at the clock and said, "You said we were going to stop at 2:15, and we only have five more minutes."

As Candace was getting ready to leave, I suggested that she think about a different way of talking to herself. When I asked her what she might say to herself now, she responded, "Candace *can* remember!" Later, I met with Candace's teacher and parents, showed them how to help Candace use her cognitive structures to remember, and encouraged them to say only positive statements to her about her ability to remember.

Many times students try to rely on short-term memory and equate it with learning. The short-term memory can hold only a small amount of information at one time. When students forget, they probably haven't processed the information. Some instructional practices drill information, hoping it will eventually stick. This kind of rote learning rarely transfers to other applications and can be recalled only when directly cued in relation to the way it was input. Practice with understanding is essential for effective memorization.

Brian: Memorizing Spelling Words

Brian, a 5th grader, was frustrated. Despite hours of review and drill every night, Brian failed every spelling test. His parents and teacher were frustrated. They did not understand why he couldn't remember words from one day to the next. Brian worked very hard and often reached the point of discouragement and tears. He was convinced that spelling was just impossible for him, and he made every effort to avoid the unpleasant task. When I started to work with him, he had a mental and emotional block to spelling. We did a number of visual, auditory, and rhythm activities to first demonstrate that he could remember things. He was very good at remembering phone numbers, songs, and raps. We looked at the spelling words. I pointed to *pioneer,* the first word on the list, and asked him to read it to me and tell me what it meant. "Pioneer. It . . . it means . . . I know I've heard it before. . . ." He paused and looked at me for clues. "I can't remember."

Brian had heard the word, but he was unsure of the meaning. We discussed the meaning until he was able to connect it to his early American social studies lessons and to programs on TV, such as *Little House on the Prairie.* Although I explained that there were other ways to be a pioneer, such as space exploration or medical discoveries, he was more familiar with historical use of the term.

"Close your eyes and picture what you see when you think of the word *pioneer,*" I prompted.

Brian closed his eyes and smiled. "I see me standing by a log cabin with my horse tied to a post," he said. "I just finished chopping wood for the fireplace. . . ."

He would have gone on, but I interrupted him, asking him to look at the word and spell it out loud. He did. Brian found it easy and enjoyable to use his imagination to picture the meaning of the word as he said it.

"Now," I said, "look at the word and tell me what you notice."

He was confused. "It just says *pioneer*."

I asked him to look at the word and spell it to make sure he was inputting every letter. When I asked what he noticed, he looked at me, hoping I would tell him what I wanted to hear. I encouraged Brian to just keep looking at it until he noticed something. This approach was new to him. At first, he tried to guess what I wanted him to say. Again, I encouraged him to trust himself and see what he noticed. Then, to his own surprise, he began to notice some interesting things about the word.

Brian hesitated and looked at me to see if he was doing it right. "There are four vowels in the word. . . . It starts with a consonant . . . then there are two vowels, a consonant, two more vowels, and then another consonant." He was now sitting on the edge of his seat looking intently at the word.

"What else do you notice?" I prompted.

"Hmm . . . pi-o-neer," he slowly pronounced the word. "It has three syllables."

"What do you notice about the syllables?"

Brian noticed aloud that every syllable had a vowel. He also noticed that one syllable—the second one—was a vowel by itself. I encouraged him to tap the syllables with his finger as he sounded them out. He looked up at me and spelled "pi-o-neer." He was surprised and delighted. I told him to close his eyes and spell it. Without hesitation, he closed his eyes and spelled the word. As he did this, he was reflectively aware and visualizing while comparing the sound of the letters with the sight of the word.

Once Brian was able to transform the word into mental representation, he was able to carry it in his mind and recall the information as needed. He noticed the other words and could not believe how easy it was to remember the spelling. Brian discovered how to use his cognitive structures to learn, create, and change. He no longer had to rely on short-term memory and be afraid of forgetting. Brian was much more confident, relaxed, and eager to learn more words.

Suggestions for Practice

1. *Encourage students to memorize with understanding* to build a database for future reference. Provide opportunities for students to ask questions. Make sure they know the meaning of words and math facts. Memorizing becomes easier with practice and the practical application of information.

2. *Play memory games,* making it fun to memorize poems, songs, facts, and skills. Give practical examples of useful information for memorization.

3. *Listen when students ask why* they need to know something. Make sure they know why they are learning names, dates, and places—not just to score well on a test but to have points of reference in a historical or geographical context. Encourage students to value memorization as a powerful cognitive structure that will build their confidence and make learning easier.

4. *Encourage students to notice things* and gather as much relevant information as possible to make connections with prior knowledge and experience. Stimulate creative investigation for self-learning. Resist the temptation to tell them what to notice.

5. *Encourage students to be reflectively aware* of what their senses are telling them. This brings information to a conscious level for processing and enhances memory.

6. *Encourage students to close their eyes and use their powerful imaginations to visualize* information they want to remember and plan how they will recall it when needed (retrace connections for access). Pictures are usually easier to remember than words. The more vivid the images, the more likely students are to rememeber them.

7. *Encourage students to attach feelings to what they want to memorize.* Provide pleasurable experiences when students need to remember something.

8. *Provide opportunities for multisensory, hands-on experiences* that apply what needs to be remembered. Students learn best by doing.

9. *Encourage students to use association strategies* such as mnemonics, acrostics, rhythms, rhymes, concept mapping, outlining, sequencing, cartooning, and contextual referencing to make memorizing easier. They can also design creative, humorous arrangements to aid memory.

10. *Encourage students to systematically rehearse and practice what they want to remember and to review their connective pathways for access.* Ask them how they would teach what they know to someone else.

... 4 ...

Conservation of Constancy

Jeff scowled as he slouched in the chair and crossed his arms to let me know he wasn't going to be forced into doing anything. This 7th grader's defiant attitude and disrespect got on the nerves of every teacher. He rarely completed assignments and was failing most of his subjects. Without much ado, I put two balls of green clay in front of Jeff and asked him to make sure they were equal in amount. He looked up at me with surprise; he had been expecting me to talk about his behavior and poor grades. Then, after a suspicious glance at me, he began to mold the clay in his hands, testing its size and weight.

I asked him to smash one ball flat, and he did. Then I asked, "Which piece of clay has more? Or do both have the same amount of clay?"

Jeff pointed to the flat piece and said, "This one has more."

I asked him to press a hole in the ball of clay. "Do you still have the same amount of clay in this ball, more clay, or less clay?"

Without hesitation he said, "Less clay, 'cause it's got a hole in it."

With this task and several others, Jeff demonstrated his need to develop the cognitive structure of conservation of constancy.

Conservation of Constancy Defined

Conservation of constancy is the ability to understand how some attributes or characteristics of a thing can change while others stay the same. *Conservation* means preservation or protection and is commonly used in the context of nature. *Constancy* means staying the same, not changing. Material things that change physically can be reversed; that is, they hold constant (conserve) some characteristics while changing others. For example, while the amount and color of Jeff's clay stayed the same, the physical shape changed but could be returned to its original form. There was no chemical change.

Conservation of constancy is a comparative cognitive structure essential for identifying relationships and making sense of physical and abstract information. Although there are many different kinds of physical conservation activities, the most common are conservation of *amount,* conservation of *volume,* conservation of *length,* conservation of *weight,* conservation of *area,* and conservation of *number.*

Although all educators study Piaget's writing on conservation, they rarely see practical application of his examples and may not grasp how critical conservation is for instruction and learning in every content area. Students who lack the ability to use this cognitive structure are easily confused and fail to benefit from their experiences. Because their perceptions are limited to concrete sensory data and literal interpretations, they try to force information to fit into preconceived notions rather than processing to learn, create, and change. This makes abstract thinking and planning very challenging. They have difficulty transferring information from one situation to another and discerning relevance because disconnected bits of data appear to be equally important.

Curriculum content, activities, and assessments in every subject area assume students can conserve constancies. Here are just a few subject-specific examples of where it is required:

- *Math*—equations, measurements, operations, word problems, data analysis, and probability
- *Language arts*—reading, writing, vocabulary, spelling, grammar, and literature
- *Social studies*—time periods, cultures, geographical data, economics, and political systems
- *Science*—experimentation with physical, organic, and chemical relationships

Helping Students Develop Conservation of Constancy

If children have mediation and are reflectively aware, they develop conservation very early. Piaget said children would normally develop conservation by age 7 or 8. However, my experience has shown me that there are many early teens who, like Jeff, have not developed this cognitive structure.

When we were growing up, we developed basic conservation of constancy by helping around the house and playing with objects that could be physically moved around, like blocks, sand, or Play-Doh. When we helped bake a cake, for example, we learned that one-quarter cup of milk poured from a measuring cup was still one-quarter cup of milk when it was in the bowl. Today, most cakes are bought ready-made from the store, and students spend more and more of their free time passively watching others do things on TV or engaging in "virtual" play via computers and gaming systems. As a result, many do not get the physical, sensory input needed to develop a basic cognitive structure like conservation of constancy. Electronic media and virtual experiences do have value and can be effective tools for developing some cognitive structures and learning new information, especially at the abstract level, once basic cognitive structures are operational. However, all students—young ones especially—need "real," tangible experience with manipulatives. A student who cannot understand physical conservation has difficulty understanding abstract conservation needed for math and reading. Some may maintain passing or even good grades by memorizing information; however, they can't connect, apply, or transfer the information to other situations. When they cannot compare how things are alike and different, each bit of data is new information.

To read, students have to be able to compare what changes and what stays the same. An *a* is still an *a* if it is capitalized or lowercase; written in manuscript printing, in cursive writing, or typed; pronounced long, short, or with other variations; and located in the beginning, middle, or end of the word (see Figure 4.1). As adults, we take this for granted. The complexity of differentiating all the shapes, sounds, and positions of a single letter can be very challenging, and the different combinations of letters can be overwhelming for students who have not developed this cognitive structure.

Figure 4.1	Variations in the Letter *A*	
Shapes	**Sounds**	**Word Position**
A **A** *a* a *a* ɑ	Long (cake) Short (cat) Blended (what, fall, car, paw)	Beginning Middle End

In reading, students without conservation of constancy cannot see what changes and what stays the same when a prefix or suffix is added to a word. When presented with *paint, painting,* and *repaint,* for example, these students will see three totally different words. The key to understanding conservation is identifying the relationship between attributes that are constant and attributes that change.

Once the nature and operation of conservation of constancy are understood, it is easy to find many different ways to mediate development of this cognitive structure. Here is an example of how I worked with Tony, who could not read.

Tony and the Folded Jacket

By February of his 1st grade year, Tony had memorized a few sight words but was still unsure of the names and sounds of some letters. We started with simple tasks, such as making and smashing balls of clay, to assess his conservation of constancy. He enjoyed playing with clay because he didn't think it had anything to do with reading. We did many variations of this task, and his responses demonstrated his lack of conservation. For example, he rolled clay into a snake shape and then coiled it, insisting there was more clay when the snake was straight. So I tried a different approach using his jacket.

First I asked Tony to take his jacket off and lay it flat on the table. After he did that, I asked if the jacket fit him. Tony looked at me to see if this was some kind of trick. Then he said it did. I asked him to fold the jacket in half and then asked, "Does the jacket fit you?" Tony said it didn't.

I asked him to open the jacket flat on the table again. "Does the jacket fit you?"

"Yes."

"Fold the jacket in half." He did. "Does the jacket fit you?" I asked again.

"No," Tony said.

"Put the jacket on." He did. "Does the jacket fit you?"

Tony adjusted the jacket, feeling very comfortable in it. "Uh huh."

We repeated the sequence. At my request, Tony took off the jacket, put it on the table, and, at my prompt, answered that yes, it fit him. Then, again at my request, he folded the jacket in half. "Does the jacket fit you?"

Tony stopped, looked at the jacket for a long moment, and put his hands together. Then he gestured as if folding the jacket and responded excitedly, "It wouldn't matter if it was folded, rolled, or anything! It would still fit me!"

This was an important moment for Tony. He suddenly realized that some things change and some things stay the same—the jacket was still the same size and would fit him even if it were folded and appeared smaller. We went back to the clay and other activities. He laughed and said, "It's still the same amount of clay, no matter what you do! You didn't add any or take any away!"

I then took one of Tony's 1st grade reading books and put it in front of him. He opened it with his usual hesitation because he knew reading was hard for him. As he looked at the first page, his facial expression changed. He pointed to the first sentence and said excitedly, "Here's 'Chip'!" He scanned the page and pointed, "Here's 'Chip' again!" He looked at the next page, "Here it is again!" He went back to the first sentence and read, "This is Chip." He looked at me proudly.

Using the sight words he had memorized, and sounding out the ones he was unsure of, Tony started to read for the first time. Although he needed help with a few new vocabulary words, he had taken a giant step toward becoming a reader. As he learned each new word, he was able to recognize it as the same word when he saw it again in a different place on the page. Using conservation of constancy, he could modify some things (in this case, the location of the word) while holding something else constant (the word itself). He was so excited when he left that his feet were hardly touching the floor. Tony was starting to develop a valuable cognitive structure that would help him make sense of information.

Individuals who haven't developed conservation of constancy are often unaware of this and even unaware that they need it. Let's take a look at some examples.

Conservation of Amount and Length

Frankie, a 7th grader, refused to do schoolwork, saying it was boring and stupid. His teachers said that he was lazy and unmotivated. When Frankie and I started with conservation activities, he was glad we weren't doing what he termed "school stuff." After pressing one of the balls of clay into a pancake, he confidently said it had more clay than the round ball. I gave him two equally long straws. After he made sure they were the same length, I moved one a little to the right. He said the straw that was moved was longer. After he experimented with many different positions, he tossed the straws on the table and said confidently, "No matter what you do with them, they are still the same length." Frankie paused, looked over at the two pieces of clay and said, "They are still the same amount of clay when you move them around, too." He sat up and thought for a minute, just looking at the straws and the clay. It was interesting to watch him processing what had just happened. He tapped his fingers on the desk, looked at me, and then sat back with a big sigh of relief.

During this and the following three sessions, we did a variety of puzzle-type activities to assess and mediate Frankie's conservation of constancy. We also looked at his classroom assignments to see how he could use conservation of constancy to identify what was changing and what was staying the same. After our second session, Frankie's language arts teacher stopped me in the hall to tell me that Frankie had turned in his first completed assignment of the year.

Once students understand conservation of constancy with physical materials, they are better equipped to use this cognitive structure with mental representations of more abstract information. Conservation is also needed for social studies, language arts, science, the arts, and all areas of life. Conservation of numbers is essential for math.

Conservation of Number

Madelyn, a 1st grader, had difficulty understanding numbers. I placed 7 black checkers in a row, with a little space between each one, and then gave Madelyn a pile of 10 red checkers. I asked her to match one of her checkers with each one of my checkers. She carefully put one of her checkers on top of each of mine. Then I asked her what she noticed. "I have some left over," she replied.

I asked her to put the extra checkers away, then put her seven red checkers in a pile. She bunched them together. After I spread my seven black checkers in a line, with three inches between each, I asked, "Who has more checkers now, or do we have the same number of checkers?"

Madelyn looked carefully at her pile and at my line of checkers. "You have more!"

"Why?" I asked.

Madelyn stretched her arms out. "Because yours are bigger!"

I did not correct Madelyn or explain to her that her response was incorrect. Instead, I asked her to experiment with many different arrangements of matching sets until she realized the number stayed the same even when arrangements differed.

Without conservation of numbers, students do not understand relationships such as $3 + 4 = 7$, $4 + 3 = 7$, $34 + 43 = 77$, $\frac{6}{12} = \frac{1}{2}$, and $1x = 2y$. Each problem or bit of information appears as disconnected data, which is overwhelming for them. They may get 100 percent on their math papers by imitating samples or memorizing facts and operations without understanding any of what they are doing.

Conservation of Weight

I have also encountered adults who needed to develop their conservation. Marsha, a teacher in one of my seminars, said she went to the post office to mail some papers. She asked the clerk for a letter-sized envelope, handed her the papers, and asked her to weigh them so she would know the cost. The clerk said she couldn't do that because the papers might weigh more when they were folded in the envelope. The clerk needed to develop conservation of weight.

Conservation of Volume

One day, as I was doing a presentation on conservation of volume for preservice teachers at a local university, a young man said, "You know, I work at a bar part-time on weekends. When I started, I could not for the life of me understand how five ounces of liquor in one shape of glass was still five ounces when I poured it into a different-shaped glass! I had to pour it back and forth until I convinced myself that it was still the same amount!"

A young woman in the audience nodded in agreement. "I work as a waitress," she said, "and I get that all the time. I serve someone beer in a glass, and they say they want it in a mug because they get more. I go back to the counter and pour the same glass of beer into a mug—it's the exact same amount, but the customer thinks it's more!"

Conservation of Area

When I was working with Cullen, a 5th grader, I placed two equal-sized sheets of green paper on the table and asked him, "What do you notice?"

"Two green pieces of paper," Cullen responded.

I told Cullen we would pretend that the green pieces of paper were fields. One piece of green paper was his field and one was mine. Then I pulled out two matching sets of three brown-paper shapes and said we were going to put some buildings on our fields. Cullen arranged his three brown-paper buildings on the green paper first, then I placed my buildings in a different arrangement (see Figure 4.2).

"Who has more grass to cut?" I asked.

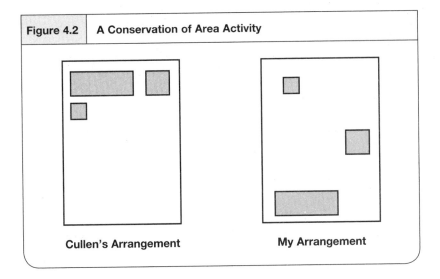

Figure 4.2   A Conservation of Area Activity

Cullen's Arrangement

My Arrangement

Cullen was puzzled and carefully studied the paper arrangements before responding hesitantly, "I would have more grass to cut."

"Why?"

"Because there is more space here," he said, pointing to the unoccupied area.

We moved our equal-size buildings in different arrangements, but Cullen still could not understand that the area covered and uncovered would be the same even if the positions of the brown-paper shapes changed. In math class, he also had difficulty with geometry; in social studies, he had a hard time reading maps.

Conservation of Constancy Is Basic

Without conservation of constancy, students also have difficulty discerning what is real and what is merely media—TV, computer, movie, and virtual representations. Interacting with students by asking questions about what they notice helps students gain more from their experience by encouraging reflective awareness.

Reflective awareness and visualization promote development of cognitive structures and metability.

When teachers learn about students' need to develop skill with a basic cognitive structure such as conservation of constancy, they come to me in disbelief, wondering, "Where do we start?" The good news is that we can use everyday lessons to help students develop conservation of constancy by encouraging them to notice what changes and what stays the same. Once teachers understand the basic principles involved in conservation of constancy and how it empowers students to construct meaning, they can use every content area to help students develop expertise with cognitive structures.

Suggestions for Practice

Any activity that changes a physical characteristic that can be reversed without chemical change will help students develop conservation of constancy. If the student cannot explain what changes and what stays the same at the physical level, he or she has difficulty processing abstract concepts. It is important for students to do conservation activities and not just watch an adult demonstrate. Encourage students to repeat and experiment with activities on their own until they realize what changes and what stays the same. It is OK to ask students why they respond the way they do. It is not OK to tell them how they should respond. Be aware that students are very keen observers of nonverbal cues and sometimes change their responses based on adult reactions. After each response, whether correct or incorrect, ask, "Why?" Activities can be done with individuals and with groups.

   1. *Conservation of volume*
- Fill two identical water bottles with tapered tops half full. Ask the student to make sure the bottles have the same amount of water. With lids on, turn one bottle upside down. Ask, "Which bottle has more water, or do

they have the same amount of water?" Ask, "Why?" If the student understands conservation of constancy, he or she will say that both bottles have the same amount because you did not add any or take any away. If the student does not understand conservation of constancy, he or she will say that one has more water.

• Have students tie a string on a ball of clay and lower the ball into a half-filled glass of water; then put a rubber band on the glass to mark the level of water. When they remove the ball of clay again and the water level drops below the rubber band, they can see how much water the clay displaced. Have students take the ball of clay and roll it into a skinny snake shape. Ask students, "If you put the snake into the water, will the water rise to the same level or be higher or lower than the rubber band?" Ask, "Why?" Have students then lower the clay snake into the water and notice what happens. Student can experiment with variations of this activity.

2. *Conservation of amount*

• Take a candy bar (or cracker, cookie, or piece of bread) and have the student break it into several pieces. Then ask, "Do you still have the same amount of candy, more, or less than you started with?" Ask, "Why?" You can also use two identical candy bars, break one, and compare it with the unbroken one.

• Take two balls of clay of exactly the same amount. Ask the student to press one ball into a pancake. Ask, "Do the pieces of clay have the same amount of clay, more clay, or less clay?" Ask, "Why?" You can vary this activity in many ways; for example, take one ball of clay and ask the student to press a hole (indentation) into the clay. Then ask, "Do you have the same amount of clay you started with, more clay, or less clay?" You can roll the clay into a fat snake, then coil the snake, and ask the same question.

• Have the student take a piece of paper and fold it or crumple it into a ball. Then ask, "Do you still have the same amount of paper you started with, more paper, or less paper?" Ask, "Why?"

3. *Conservation of length*

• Give students two straws or sticks that are exactly the same length and have them confirm that they are equal. Lay them side by side. Move one stick about two inches to the right. Ask, "Which stick is longer, or are they the same length?" Ask, "Why?" There are many variations you can do with sticks: stand one on end and leave the other one laying on the table; form a *T* or *X* with them; ask the student to hold one behind his or her back. Repeat the same question. After the student responds (whether correctly or incorrectly) to each change of position, ask the student to lay the two sticks side by side and compare them, again confirming that they are the same length, before changing position.

• Take a rope or string and lay it out straight; then lay it in a wavy line or tie it in a loose knot and ask, "Is the rope still the same length, longer, or shorter than it was when you started?" Ask, "Why?" Again, you can do this with one rope or with two ropes of the same length. If you use two ropes, move one and leave the other straight for comparison.

• Lay two strips of paper, exactly the same length, side by side. Place toy cars (or blocks to represent cars) on one end of each strip of paper. Ask, "If the paper is a road and the cars are identical and are going exactly the same speed, which car would come to the end of the road first, or would they come to the end at the same time?" Ask, "Why?" Remove the cars and move one strip ahead a little. Place the cars on the strips and ask the same questions.

4. *Conservation of weight*
   - Weigh two equal balls of clay or play dough. Flatten one into a pancake and ask, "Which one will weigh more now, or will they weigh the same?" Ask, "Why?" Weigh the pieces again. You can also use stacked and unstacked blocks or any object that can be weighed whole and then broken into pieces.

5. *Conservation of number*
   - Place two sets of counters in two rows side by side to demonstrate that they are equal matching sets. Move counters in one row far apart and group the other row into a pile. Ask, "Which set of counters has more and which has less, or do they have the same amount?" Ask, "Why?"
   - Take two sets of identical rectangular blocks. Lay three horizontally side by side and stand three vertically. Ask, "Which group of blocks has more or do they have the same number?" Ask, "Why?" Stack three horizontally and three vertically. Ask the same questions.

6. *Conservation of area*
   - Take two sheets of equal-sized paper. Ask the student to pretend that they are pieces of property. Have two matching sets of equal-size objects or cut-out shapes. Give the student one set to place on his or her paper; then place identical objects on your paper in different locations. Ask, "Whose blocks cover more paper?" or "Which paper has more unused area (or paper)?" Ask, "Why?" Repeat with variations.

7. *Conservation of constancy*
   - Ask students to identify when they need conservation of constancy in school and everyday life.
   - Ask yourself or the students: How is conservation of constancy needed for this lesson? How can I use this lesson to develop conservation of constancy?

··· 5 ···

Classification

Carmen, a 3rd grader, was eager to learn but easily frustrated, and she often disrupted the class with outbursts of anger. I placed small plastic flowers on the table in front of Carmen: five roses and three tulips. I asked Carmen what she saw, and her response was, "A bunch of flowers."

"What do you notice?" I prompted.

"Some are roses and some are tulips."

"How are they all alike in some way?" I asked.

"They're all flowers? Oh, and they're all plastic!" Carmen offered.

"OK. How many roses are there?"

Carmen moved the roses around and counted them as she did so: "One–two–three–four–five."

I made a note to myself that Carmen's physically moving the flowers suggested that she could not visualize the information. "How many tulips are there?" I asked.

Once again, Carmen touched as she counted: "One–two–three."

"Are there more roses or more flowers?" I asked her.

Without hesitation, she responded, "More roses."

Carmen was not seeing roses as part of the larger set of flowers. To her, roses were roses, tulips were tulips, and flowers were flowers. She needed to develop the cognitive structure of classification.

Classification Defined

Classification involves identifying, comparing, and ordering information or data to create meaning based on relationships of parts to each other and parts to the whole. To classify, students need to apply criteria for belonging or not belonging to a group or set.

There are three basic ways to use categories to organize information:

1. *Uni-classification* focuses on the unique attributes of a particular object, person, or bit of information. For example, a box has attributes such as color, shape, size, weight, and function.

2. *Set–subset classification* identifies relationships of parts to each other and to the whole. For example, classrooms, halls, and offices are part of a school building; country, ZIP code, state, city, number, and name are subcategories of an address.

3. *Set-to-set classification* compares and contrasts differing elements of related sets. For example, single-family houses are compared with multiple-unit apartments in terms of cost, style, or location; test scores are compared with national percentiles, standards, or other sets of scores.

Every classification system depends on the nature of the elements being classified. Identified criteria, or standards, determine membership in a group or set.

Criteria for classification can be physical or abstract. Here are examples of criteria:

• *Kind or type* classifies elements according to common traits within a named group such as "utilities" or "gender." Standardized classification systems are used in the sciences;

biology, for example, uses kingdom, phylum, class, order, family, genus, and species. Common nouns (those that are not proper or individual names) make up a category that classifies the kind of noun.

• *Purpose* classifies how a product or activity fulfills what it was designed to do; for example, things that heat for cooking, such as a stove; things that process information, such as a computer; and things that transport people, such as cars and airplanes.

• *Rank order* classifies a series of elements in relationship to ascending or descending order; for example, relative size from largest to smallest, quantification from most to least, alphabetical order, priorities based on what has to be completed first, and hierarchies within social systems.

• *Degree* classifies elements according to relative intensity of such things as conditions, feelings, level or extent of success, cognitive engagement, and motivation. Degree is based on a continuum of capacity or level of possibility; an example would be chemicals or situations that are dangerous, more dangerous, or the most dangerous.

• *Frequency or probability* classifies elements or variables according to how many times something occurs or is likely to occur within a given period of time or how often a single element appears within a specific group or category; examples would be the number of home runs hit by a baseball player in a single season and a person's attendance rate at work or school.

• *Level of precision* classifies accuracy of data, measurement, construction, or performance, in other words, quality of work compared to a standard of excellence. For examples, grades and test scores in school are often based on levels of correctness, and surgeons develop levels of expertise.

Language provides labels for classifying and communicating; however, it is not enough to simply tell students the names of items. They need to reflect on and visualize sensory information to make it their own; recognize a fit with prior knowledge and experience so they can memorize this information for ready recall; and use conservation of constancy to compare how the variables of items are alike and different. Classification works with other cognitive structures to develop the ability to learn, create, and change.

Classification affects all aspects of learning and life. National and international agencies are dedicated to collecting, analyzing, and disseminating information about the field of classification, which includes such methods as multidimensional scaling, numerical taxonomies, clustering, network models, and routing. Social, economic, and political organizations classify services, information, resources, and interactions. Imagine if grocery stores, libraries, and the postal service did not use classification systems. In schools, too, content areas are classified in terms of standards, scope, and sequence to organize what has to be taught at each grade level. Computers process and classify relationships between entities by using logical operators such as *and, or,* and *not* to identify members of sets or on–off computer circuit elements. The more effectively students use classification to process information, the more accessible and useful that information is for them.

Helping Students Develop Classification

Students are accustomed to hearing from their teachers how texts and other information are classified. For example, a teacher might call their attention to a book's table of contents, headings, or other key features. It would be more effective for the teacher to ask these students, "What do you notice about how the book (text, data, information) is organized?" or "Why do you think the information is classified this way?"

As I worked with students from all grade levels, I observed that in some subjects, they tended to encounter the same content year after year. Punctuation, for example, is taught from 1st grade on, and yet the upper grade teachers complain that students still make common errors. Although students are taught the information and complete plenty of exercises and tests, it's likely they never identify a classification system they can use to identify criteria for using punctuation correctly and truly make this content their own. I encourage teachers to give the students a text and have them find punctuation patterns and generate rules based on classification of the data. This helps students create meaning for themselves, changing their understanding of content and learning when, where, and how to use punctuation correctly rather than just memorizing rules and completing worksheets.

To use the curriculum to help students develop cognitive structures, teachers need to analyze content, instruction, and assessment by asking these two questions:

1. To make sense of this information, what do the students have to be able to classify?

2. How can I use this lesson to help students develop the cognitive structure of classification?

Frequently, we assume that students effectively use cognitive structures to process information we present in class. Without realizing it, we tell them what they need to classify and how to do it so that they can complete an assignment. However, when we give them the criteria for organizing information, we are doing the work for them and depriving them of opportunities to use cognitive structures and develop metability.

For example, in a science experiment, teachers often give detailed instructions including expected outcomes, identify categories for variables, and set up the worksheet for recording results. The students follow directions with little or no personal investment or processing of information. The same experiment or activity can be used to develop classification skills by giving students materials and safety instructions and encouraging them to notice and document their observations as they collect and classify the data for analysis and interpretation. Students will gain expertise using the cognitive structure of classification if they come up with the criteria by identifying the relationships of parts to each other and parts to the whole.

A music teacher tried every year to have students remember the basic information needed to read music. After learning about cognitive structures, she redesigned her lessons to help students develop classification. She had students work in small groups to make little cards with note shapes, note names, symbols, staff positions, rhythms, keys, scales, intervals, chords, and so on. When they finished, she asked them to organize and reorganize the cards into categories and explain why they grouped them together. They enjoyed doing the activity *and* they remembered the information.

Language arts teachers can have students identify and classify characteristics of good writing and evaluate their own writing by comparing it with specific criteria. To help students identify and understand parts of speech, teachers can distribute a text and ask them to classify how the words they find are alike in some way. Students will probably make many mistakes when they start doing these types of activities, but by defining categories and criteria for membership in a category, they are developing the cognitive structure of classification. This kind of learning has meaning because it is created by the students and changes the way they process and use information. They are using their cognitive structures to develop metability.

One of the first questions I ask students is *"What do you wish you understood better?"* Their response immediately tells me about their reflective awareness and their ability to classify information. If they know what they know, then they also know what they do not know or need to know. If they are unsure what they know, everything is vague and confusing for them. Here is an example of how I worked with a student to help him develop classification.

Greg: Making Shapes His Own

Greg was a 6th grader frequently heard to mutter, "I hate school!" All through school, he depended on memorization and imitation to complete enough work to barely get by. In class, he said he was bored or the work was stupid rather than asking for help. Because he had a history of failure and frustration, I started with a hands-on classification activity.

Without any instructions, I put an assortment of brightly colored paper shapes on the table: circles, triangles, rectangles, squares, and a few odd shapes. Each shape was represented in three sizes and in three colors. At first Greg sat there looking bored. After a long pause, I asked him what he could do with the pieces of paper. "Throw them away," Greg responded. When I asked him why, he said, "They're not good for anything. It's just a bunch of paper." Then I asked what he noticed about the paper. He began to casually move pieces around and noted that there were four colors. When Greg looked at the pieces of paper, he used blurred and sweeping perception and made a snap judgment that cut off sensory input. So I prompted him to tell me what else he noticed. He fiddled disinterestedly with the paper and commented that there were some shapes. I asked Greg to tell me more, and he picked up a large blue circle. "Here's a circle." Then, Greg pointed to a blue square and a blue rectangle and said, "I get these mixed up."

"What about them do you know for sure?" I asked him.

"Well, they're kind of square," he commented.

Then I asked Greg to tell me how the two shapes were alike and different. He pointed to a rectangle and said, "This one has shorter sides and longer sides."

"What else do you notice?" I asked him.

He picked up a square and said, "This one . . . this one, the sides look like they're all the same length."

With more prompting about what else he noticed, Greg held up a blue rectangle and a blue square and observed that they were both blue. Then he said that they both had pointy corners. I commented that he had noticed a lot and asked if he'd like to know what the corners are called. Greg nodded and smiled sheepishly. "Yeah, but I will probably forget."

Then I asked Greg if he would like to learn how to let his mind work for him to make learning easier. "I hate school!" Greg responded. "Everything is so hard!" Then he tossed the shapes back on the table, folded his arms, and leaned back in his chair.

Greg was dealing with years of repeated failure. Although he was physically present in school, he had dropped out mentally in the early grades. He was resigned to just suffering through as best he could. Without even being aware of it, Greg had labeled everything related to schoolwork as hard. He was not yet a behavior problem, but his level of confusion, frustration, and anger were predictors of future troubles. He was mentally and emotionally disengaged with school.

Since 1st grade, Greg's teachers and parents had told him the names of shapes many times, and Greg would repeat these names, using his short-term memory. However, he never abstracted the criteria for classifying how and why shapes were alike and different. I encouraged him to stick with me and see if he could learn to use his mental tools to make learning easier. He agreed.

Next, I picked up a square and pointed to a corner, explaining that it was called a square corner, a right angle, or a 90-degree angle. "Oh, yeah," he said. "I've heard those before, but I didn't know what it meant." I took out a protractor and two rulers, and I asked him if he knew what a 180 was in skateboarding. "Yeah, that's when you flip all the way around and go the opposite direction," he responded, demonstrating with his hands. "I'm good at that!" he said, smiling.

I acknowledged Greg's ability and interest. I then explained that when lines curved or bent at a corner, we couldn't measure the curve with a ruler, so we used degrees. I showed him a protractor, and after asking him what he observed, I gave him two rulers and asked him to make a 90-degree angle. He crossed the rulers and laid them perpendicular to each other on the protractor. Again, I asked him what he noticed.

Greg looked at the rulers, as if for the first time. He pointed and said, "I made one, two, three, four 90-degree angles."

Next I asked Greg to find some 90-degree angles in the room. He looked around, got up, and pointed out the top corner of a file cabinet, the corner of a drawer, label holders, a door, a picture frame, and so on. "Wow! They're everywhere!" he said.

This was a new experience. Although Greg had seen 90-degree angles all his life, he had never consciously noticed them or classified them. As he sat back down, he had a whole different attitude. He picked up a rectangle and square and held them side by side. "These both have 90-degree angles on their corners. They both have four 90-degree angles." Then he held up the square. "But this one has all the same length sides. This one is a square?" He questioned himself and looked to me for confirmation that he had the correct name for the shape.

I smiled and assured him that he did. Then I picked up a large blue triangle and asked, "What do you notice about this shape? What do you notice about the corners or angles?"

Greg picked up the shape, moved it around in his fingers, and said he didn't think the angles were 90 degrees. I asked him how he could find out. He thought for a minute, placed the triangle on the square, then picked it up and tried to line up its corners with the rulers that were still laying on the protractor. "Nope! These are not 90 degrees. They are not square corners."

Pointing to the square, I asked him what he noticed about the sides. He asked what I meant. "Look at the sides or edges of the square and compare them to the edges of a circle," I prompted.

"Oh, these edges are straight," he said, running his finger along the sides of a square. Then he pointed to the circle and said, "Those edges are curved."

I then asked Greg to close his eyes and picture a square in his mind. When he did, he said audibly to himself, "Squares have four 90-degree angles and four sides the same length. Oh, and the sides are all straight." He nodded his head as he spoke, as if reassuring himself.

Greg was able to use his imagination to visualize sensory data and classify how shapes were alike and different. During our interaction, I had to resist the temptation to simply tell him the square had four equal straight sides and four 90-degree angles. When I share this example with teachers, some express a little impatience and say that Greg "should already have known that stuff." My response is that no matter how much or how often we teach "that stuff," students don't know it until they process the information and make it their own. It was by becoming aware of sensory information and mentally representing it that Greg was able to use classification to process the information and change his understanding to create learning. Even though he had seen and heard about 90-degree angles and squares for years, he had never used classification as a cognitive structure to identify what they were and what they were not. My approach with Greg took longer than simply retelling the features of a square, but it was the one that worked.

Over the years I have learned to ask open-ended questions that encourage students to gather and process more data. For example, instead of just telling Greg that the angles of the triangle were not 90 degrees, I asked him how he could find out. Once students begin noticing and identifying elements of the learning situation, teachers can clarify and extend that learning by sharing more information. This way, students have something to connect with, and they are motivated and invested in the process.

As much as we would like to have students on grade level, we have to analyze their level of understanding and take them where they are. I have found that students usually need to start with very simple exercises that build their sense of competence, provide practice using cognitive structures, and fill in gaps in their knowledge base.

With that goal in mind, Greg and I continued to work with the shapes to further develop his ability to classify information. Because he now recognized what a square was, I asked him to compare a square with a rectangle shape. He hesitantly identified the rectangle by name. By comparing the two shapes, he was able to identify how they were alike (90-degree angles) and different (the length of the sides). Then Greg more confidently pulled out squares and rectangles of different colors and sizes and grouped them into piles by shape. From that step, he was able to group all the circles together and all the triangles together. Then he held up one of the odd shapes. "I don't know what these are called," Greg said.

"What do they look like?" I asked.

"Just odd shapes. I'll put them all in this pile. There!" He stopped and looked at me, satisfied with his work.

After more questioning and thinking, Greg recognized that he had grouped the pieces of paper by shape. This was a new process for him. Greg usually thought of things in terms of specific instances or items rather than categories and subcategories. I explained that using categories would make it much easier for him to understand and remember information. I pointed to the pieces of paper and asked Greg if there were other ways he could group the items. "Nope. I got them in the right piles," he said.

I then asked him what he noticed about the pieces in the pile of squares. "They're all squares," he responded. I asked him what else he noticed. "They're different colors," he said, pausing. "Oh! I could put all the blue pieces together, all the green ones. . . ." He started moving the pieces around. Then he stopped, looked at me and said, "But now the squares and triangles, the shapes, will get all mixed up."

I waited as he sat there looking puzzled.

"Wait a minute." He paused, looking at the pieces and thinking. "This is kind of like that clay and water stuff we did. The pieces are alike in some ways and different in some ways." Greg was now sitting on the edge of his chair, totally engaged in what he was doing.

"Wow! That is exactly right! Your mind is really working now!" I said.

"OK, OK. I now have the shapes grouped by color. But look, I could also group them by size." He quickly rearranged the pieces according to size: large, medium, and small. "Wait! Wait! I could also put them by shapes that are regular, like squares, circles, rectangles, and triangles, and those that are not, like these." He pointed to the odd shapes. Then he quickly moved the papers into two groups. "And . . . and, I could make a group with only straight edges, a group with only curved edges, and a group that has both, like these odd shapes. Wow!"

"What did you learn from doing this?" I prompted.

"I can organize things lots of different ways," Greg commented.

Each time Greg made different groupings, he named the criteria. What started as a bunch of paper to throw away became a valuable tool for helping him develop classification.

After students make connections and find patterns and relationships, they need to use their cognitive structures to formulate predictable rules and abstract generalizable principles that transfer to other situations. I pointed out to Greg that he had classified the papers several different ways, and I asked him when he classified items or information in real life.

Greg leaned back in his chair, looked at me quizzically, and then sat there thinking for a long time. "I'm not real sure if this is what you mean, but at home when I help Mom put the groceries away, she always insists I put the canned food together the same. I mean, like, the soup with the soup, the canned fruit together, and stuff like that." He paused, reflecting. "In the grocery store, it's kind of like that, all the fruit together, all the meat together, all the bread. Wow! I never thought about that before!" I asked Greg why the grocery store grouped food that way, and he observed that it made it easier to find what you wanted.

To develop classification, students need to begin manipulating real objects. Only after they understand the principle of membership in a set and the relationship of parts to each other and parts to the whole can they classify more abstract information. Although Greg had successfully classified the pieces of paper, and saw some application at home, he did not yet see how classification applied to schoolwork.

When I asked him how he classified information at school, he said he had never really thought about it. "Think about science," I prompted. "How do you classify things in science?"

"I don't get it. What do you mean?" Greg asked.

Even when students are assigned specific tasks that require classification, they are often just imitating a model or following directions rather than using the task to develop cognitive structures. It is frustrating for teachers when students do not make obvious connections. Too often, we tell them how to connect or classify information rather than letting them use an experience as an opportunity for development. Once they understand how to use their cognitive structures effectively, they can apply them in many different situations, not just in the example presented. Greg had been classifying plants and animals since kindergarten, but he only did what he was told. He had no way to know for himself if his answers were correct. He just waited to see how the teacher graded his papers. And because he usually guessed, he had many errors and threw the papers away.

As our discussion continued, I asked Greg how a flower and a cat are alike and different. He wrinkled his nose and looked at me quizzically. "They are both alive?"

"How are they different?" I asked.

"One is a plant and one is an animal."

I asked him to tell me more. "Plants are like anything that grows, like trees, weeds, vegetables," he said, pausing to think. "Wait a minute. You mean *plants* is a category?"

"A category is the name of a group of things that are alike in some way," I explained.

"OK, OK. So *animals* is a kind of category, but there are lots of different kinds of animals."

"Right," I said, explaining that categories, or *sets,* contain many different subcategories, or *subsets.*

"So I could have cats that are animals, dogs that are animals, cows, pigs, whatever?" he asked.

"Exactly. Then within a set of dogs, there are many subsets of different kinds of dogs."

"Never thought of it like that," Greg said.

I explained that classifying really makes it easier to learn because we are making connections in our minds. Then we can find information when we need it because it is all connected together into categories that form patterns and relationships. Then I asked Greg to think about how he would classify information in other subjects, such as social studies.

"Social studies? I hate social studies!" Greg responded.

"Maybe it wouldn't be so hard if you organized information into categories."

"We're studying ancient history—Egypt, Rome, Greece. What's there to organize or classify?" he asked.

"What is Egypt?"

"A country."

"How is it alike and different from other countries?" I prompted.

"It's just a country."

"What makes a country a country? How is a country alike or different from a city or a continent?" I asked.

Greg laughed. "This is getting too heavy. My brain is swollen! I never had to think this much!"

"Why don't you let your mind work on these things," I suggested. "We'll talk about them again next time. Think about when and how you can classify in each class."

"I don't know if I can keep thinking this hard," Greg said. "But it *is* kinda fun."

Like so many other students, Greg really wanted to learn. He had just given up because nothing made sense. During our interaction, he experienced a little spark of hope. He discovered he really could develop his cognitive structures.

Exercises for Teachers

Teachers usually struggle to imagine what it is like for students who have underdeveloped cognitive structures. In seminars that I conduct with teachers, I include activities that help them become aware of how they process information automatically. Here's an example of a classification exercise.

I ask teachers to form groups of 4 to 6 and then to all place 8 to 10 items from their purses or pockets on the table. Without saying anything, I observe as most participants just sit there, waiting for instructions. A few begin to explore and handle the assortment of objects. I wait. They keep looking at me, expecting me to tell them what to do. One or two groups may start to sort the items. After a short time, if no one has started organizing the objects, I say to the group, "This is your life! How could you make sense of it?" Some of them look confused and ask, "What do you want us to do?" "What do you mean?" I encourage them to think about how they could organize the materials. Gradually, they begin sorting by putting keys in one pile, wallets in another, and so on. When they feel they're finished, I say, "You've sorted objects according to like kind. Now use criteria to classify them 30 to 40 different ways." They look at me with disbelief. Expressing doubt that this was possible, one participant said, "Today?"

With this activity, the participants become reflectively aware of their own cognitive processing. To classify, general criteria have to be selected, and every object has to be included. Participants usually start with obvious criteria, such as materials the objects are made of, color, weight, or texture. Then they identify many different criteria, for example, country of origin, alphabetical order based on object name, purpose, or cost. Together, they come up with 80 to 90 different ways to classify the objects. I then ask participants to discuss when, where, and how they use classification in school and in everyday life. I also ask them to think about how those experiences would be different if no classification existed. They become aware of classification and realize they cannot assume students are classifying effectively. We can encourage students to notice when and how things are classified at home, at school, in stores, on TV, in books, and so on. We can use every content area to help students develop the cognitive structure of classification.

Exercises for Parents

Parents too can use many types of activities at home to help students develop classification. It is important to provide opportunities for self-organizing by encouraging students to notice how items are alike and different and explain in their own words why they think some should be grouped together. For example, students can help with simple tasks such as putting the groceries away or organizing toys, books, CDs, DVDs, games, tools, files on the computer, photos, and more. Celebrate their efforts and successes. This is especially important when students begin to see how classifying brings order into their lives and makes it easier for them to function. Parents can start at a very early age to help their children develop classification skills by giving them diverse assortments of objects and asking them to group items that go together and tell why. Then ask them to find different ways to group the same objects and explain why. Doing these types of activities with physical (sensory) objects gives them a huge advantage when they go to school and start dealing with more abstract information.

Kathy: Changing Her Children's Jobs

Kathy was a parent attending one of my seminars. After we'd done the classification activity, Kathy said, "I just realized something! My 3rd grade daughter is doing well in school. My son in 5th grade is struggling. You know what? My daughter's jobs at home are setting the table, emptying the dishwasher, matching socks from the laundry, and things like that. She's classifying! My son's jobs are picking up the yard, feeding the dog, taking the trash out, and that kind of thing. I am going to switch their jobs and see what happens."

At our next seminar session, Kathy shared the results of her experience. "You are not going to believe this," she said. "But when I switched the kids' jobs, my son could not match the socks! It took him more than 45 minutes to figure out which ones went together. I really had to work with him on classifying things."

That was the last class in the series, and I did not hear from Kathy until four weeks later, when she came by on Parent Conference night. At that time, she showed me her son's report card, pointing out that he had brought up every subject at least one grade level. "It works!" she said. "And if I hadn't taken that class," she added, "I would never have thought about how I could help my kids develop cognitive structures!"

Suggestions for Practice

1. *Ask students, "What do you notice?"* The more sensory data they gather, the more they have to process. Encourage students to explain how objects, information, situations, words, and so on are alike and different from other things and how they are related in sets and subsets. For example, explain to a child that a car is different from a truck but they are both vehicles, and that milk

is different from juice but they are both liquids. Every noun is a category that can be divided into subcategories.

2. *Give students collections of assorted materials and ask them to put things together that go together.* Then ask them to regroup and reclassify the same materials. Do not tell them how to classify the materials. It is important that the students decide the criteria for classification. It is this process of identifying, comparing, and organizing that develops classification structures.

3. *Involve students in practical classification tasks* in everyday life. Encourage them to classify and organize their personal possessions and then to explain their criteria for the groupings.

4. *Encourage students to notice and describe classification systems in everyday life,* for example, postal addresses, phone numbers, books, content in texts, schedules, and computer searches. Ask students to explain how various elements are related to each other.

5. *Encourage students to use graphic organizers*—such as diagrams, outlines, matrices, and illustrations—to identify the relationships of parts to each other and to the whole, and the relationships of sets and subsets to each other. Instead of giving them preprinted forms, ask them to create their own format.

6. *Model classification.* Explain to students why you group items the way you do (mentally and physically). Encourage students to notice how order (organization and classification) reduces their stress, speeds their thinking and other activities, develops their efficiency, and helps them control and predict outcomes in many situations.

7. *Encourage students to be conscious of how they process abstract information,* in other words, what kinds of connections (groupings, classification) they make in their minds when they interact with new or familiar information. How do they process information for storage and retrieval? Encourage students to notice how objects or information are parts of sets and subsets (class inclusion) and the relationships of parts to each other and to the whole.

8. *Play games that involve classification and pattern finding,* for example, I Spy, 20 Questions, picture puzzles, SET (which requires identifying sets by color, shape, number, and shading), Connect Four (which involves trying to get four circles of the same color in a row), and certain computer games.

9. *Talk about and draw family relations.* This helps students see where they belong within a larger system or network of people. Encourage students to identify individuals in the family and all the possible relationships each has with other members of the family.

10. *Use time and space as criteria for organizing relationships.* Encourage students to notice when and where things and events are in relationship to each other and to the clock and calendar. This helps them classify and access information.

11. *Ask students how they might classify their belongings, at school or at home.*

···6···

Spatial Orientation

Joe was a 6th grader who couldn't seem to get it together. He regularly lost his books, homework, and personal belongings. His parents called him a mixed-up kid and were constantly telling him to watch where he was going. After a physical and visual checkup turned up no abnormalities, Joe's teachers tried behavior modification strategies, which included checklists and prizes when he had all his books. These had little lasting effect. The root cause of Joe's difficulties was a lack of spatial orientation, which affected every aspect of his personal and academic life.

After assessing Joe's spatial orientation, I decided to use an activity called Verbal Directions to help him develop his spatial cognitive structure. With a video camera recording our interaction, Joe and I sat across the table from one another with a large piece of poster board set up between us so that neither could see the other's workspace. Each of us had a matching set of blocks (we used Cuisennaire Rods). I explained to Joe that his task was to build something with his blocks and give me directions that would allow me to duplicate his construction. He did this with lots of enthusiasm.

Joe started by telling me, "Take the orange." For the purpose of the exercise, I did not ask any clarifying questions. Here, because

Joe didn't say how many orange blocks to take, I took one. He did not say where to put it, so I stood it in front of me. Then Joe said, "Take a green block and put it by the orange." There were two shades of green blocks, so I picked a dark green one and placed it by the orange block. "Take two yellow ones then two red ones," he said next. Joe did not tell me where to put the yellow or red blocks, so I held them in my hand. "Take six little white ones and line them up." I placed six little white blocks in a row.

Joe sat back and said, "Looks good, huh?"

"Well, let's see," I said, removing the poster board.

Joe's mouth dropped open. Then he frowned. "You didn't do what I told you!" he said, pointing to his arrangement of blocks, which looked nothing like mine.

As I rewound the videotape, I told Joe that I really had tried to follow his directions. We watched the playback together, and I noticed the amazement on Joe's face as he heard his vague and incomplete instructions. Although he saw where his blocks were, he never said where they were in relation to other blocks.

We went on to do the exercise several different times. Joe gave instructions for me to follow; then I gave instructions for him to follow. Because my instructions were very specific about where to place the blocks in relationship to each other, our constructions were identical. He gradually began to tell me where to put each block in relationship to other blocks.

Spatial Orientation Defined

Spatial orientation is a cognitive structure that helps individuals identify and compare where objects and places are in relationship to each other and to oneself. To understand space, students have to be aware of several things:

- Boundaries that define and differentiate one object from another.
- Relationships between and among objects.

- The difference between material objects and mental images.
- Types and characteristics of space.

Helping Students Develop Spatial Relations

To develop spatial orientation, students need to be reflectively aware of their physical position and to visualize spatial relationships among persons, places, and things when they are out of sensory range. They also need to represent and communicate relationships using language, drawings, gestures, or models.

When mediating the development of this cognitive structure, help students understand the four types of space and the four characteristics of spatial orientation that influence how they interact with information and sensory experience.

Four Types of Space

Spatial relationships provide a framework for gathering, organizing, and processing information in terms of the four types of space: *material, representational, abstract,* and *virtual.*

Material space. Material space consists of physical, material things that have three-dimensional form, occupy space, and are perceived by the senses; that is, they can be seen, touched, heard, tasted, or smelled. In my art classes, instead of teaching students *to draw,* I focused on teaching them *to see,* to notice relationships. One day I asked students to carefully observe their hands and draw them in various positions. Angie, a 7th grader, grasped her raised left wrist in her right hand and said excitedly, "Ms. Garner, it's always been there, but now I *see* it!" Many students who had never considered themselves talented or artistic were very pleased to discover that they really could draw when they noticed spatial relationships.

Classroom teachers see results when they teach their students to become reflectively aware of sensory input. Here is an example of a kindergarten teacher who mediated an experience with her students.

Mary: Studying Shadows with Her Students

Mary was teaching her kindergarten students to notice things around them. One day they were observing shadows and experimenting with flashlights to create shadows. When they discussed what they had learned, one student said, "I noticed that anything that light can't pass through has a shadow." Another said, "I noticed that if I shined two flashlights on a pencil, it had two shadows. I wonder: if there were seven lights, would there be seven shadows?" After these explorations, Mary found that her students often took the lead in their own learning by sharing what they noticed about the lesson she was teaching.

Every subject area in school assumes that students understand material spatial relationships. In physical and biological sciences, for example, students need spatial cognitive structures to gather and process sensory data about the attributes of matter and the characteristics of plants and animals—all of which occupy space. In social studies, students need spatial cognitive structures to understand geographic land masses and how these affect culture, history, politics, economics, and so on. In language arts, especially in the study of literature, students have to visualize people, places, and things described to comprehend what they are reading. In mathematics, students learn to measure, weigh, count, and analyze the physical forms of objects and materials. In music, students learn how the form of an instrument directly affects the kind of sounds it makes. In physical education, they learn how to use their bodies in relationship to each other and to equipment. Finally, in art, they use many different media to mold, sculpt, and construct form. Students are immersed in a world of three-dimensional material forms, from their own bodies to everything they come in contact with.

We can help our students develop spatial orientation by encouraging them to use reflective awareness and visualization.

Representational space. Representational space uses lines or edges to define two-dimensional shapes and symbols. Drawings, diagrams, lines, paintings, photos, and videos use shapes to represent or stand for persons, places, things, and ideas. Coding systems such as languages, numbers, and musical notations are all based on using two-dimensional spatial relationships to communicate meaning. For example, specific directional lines represent numbers and symbols. In reading and writing, the directions of lines form letters. The spacing between letters and words and the organization of words on a page form patterns for legibility. In my art classes, students often created the illusion of a three-dimensional form on a flat, two-dimensional paper using representational space. I showed the younger students how to draw geometric shapes such as squares and then add additional lines and shading to make the shapes appear three-dimensional.

When I am working with students in grades 3 through 12 and I want to quickly assess their spatial orientation, I ask them to draw floor plans, or diagrams, of their houses to show where the rooms are in relationship to each other. Figure 6.1 shows some floor plans created by 6th graders with disconnected spatial orientation. When parent and teacher groups do this exercise, I encourage participants to think about their thinking as they draw. During this process, they suddenly realize how visualization and reflective awareness make it possible for them to mentally walk through their houses and notice relationships.

If students have difficulty seeing spatial relationships in their real world, they usually have difficulty understanding representational, abstract, and virtual spatial relationships. This has far-reaching implications for learning and life. Math uses spatial representation in geometry, number systems, and trends.Science uses graphs, matrices, and diagrams to represent data. Geography and social studies integrate spatial orientation in every aspect of

Figure 6.1 | **Floor Plans Illustrating Disconnected Spatial Orientation**

study. In language arts, letters and words are based on specific shapes that have been assigned sounds and meaning. In music, notes and symbols have shapes that represent the sounds, rhythms, and tempo. In physical education, shapes are used to symbolically represent game plays, dance steps, and exercises. In art, spatial characteristics are essential elements of design.

Representational space as described here can be perceived by the senses. However, it can also be transformed through mental representation or visualization into abstract spatial relationships.

Abstract space. Abstract space uses mental images to transcend physical limitations when representing spatial relationships. For example, when planning a trip, we can mentally map going from one place to another. This ability to abstractly represent and manipulate spatial relationships is faster and more efficient than using physical or symbolic space.

For students to be successful in school, they need to use abstract spatial relationships to mentally represent things they cannot directly perceive with their senses. In science class, for example, they need to be able to visualize molecular structures, planetary orbits, speed, and motion. In mathematics, they need to "see" how theories and formulas apply to practical problem solving. In social studies, they need to picture boundaries and topography in relationship to events and culture over time. In language arts, they need to abstractly represent context and plan written and oral expression. In music, they need to mentally hear a composition or translate notation before they can perform it. In art, they need to visualize how they will organize space when they draw, paint, or construct something. And in physical education, they need to mentally practice skills and moves.

The following example shows how a teacher helped her students understand physical, representational, and abstract spatial relationships.

Barbara: Teaching Perimeter

Barbara paired the students in her 6th grade math class and gave each pair 30 one-centimeter cubes. Their challenge, she explained, was to make as many different rectangular forms as they could using all 30 cubes for each rectangle. She also asked them to draw and measure each rectangular form and thus, represent the three-dimensional shapes with two-dimensional symbols. When students exhausted ways to make rectangles, Barbara asked them to review the data they had collected and share what they noticed. The students observed that the perimeter of every configuration was the same.

With this concrete activity, Barbara helped her students understand physical, representational, and abstract spatial relationships. Too often, teachers use only symbolic or abstract representation, mistakenly assuming that all their students understand physical space.

Virtual space. Virtual space uses social or personal norms to identify spatial relationships. For example, "personal space" is a virtual boundary defined by social or cultural norms. Technology creates virtual environments to simulate reality. Computer training programs, games, and simulations may or may not be based on representations of real space. Some students, especially those who are heavily involved in video games, can develop a blurred understanding of the difference between real and virtual space. Such misperceptions negatively affect their ability to function within the context of physical space because they confuse what is outside themselves with what is in their imaginations. The projection of virtual images can interfere with their perception of sensory data. It is important to help students become reflectively aware of physical, representational, abstract, and virtual spatial relationships and how to use them to make sense of information.

Characteristics of Spatial Orientation

An individual's spatial orientation affects how that person gathers, processes, and expresses information. Although we usually think of *location, distance, direction,* and *perspective* in terms of physical relationships, they also apply to representational, abstract, and virtual space.

Location. This is the placement or position of items in space. To describe and compare locations, we use words such as *on, in, over, under, above, below, between, beside, in front of, behind, inside, outside, near, far, top, bottom, left, right, north, south, east,* and *west.* However, we cannot assume that students who use these words always understand spatial relationships.

All material things have a location or position in space. Order reduces stress and confusion by organizing items in relationship to each other. When a teacher tells a student to clean up a messy desk or reorganize the contents of a folder, these instructions are meaningless if the student doesn't have spatial orientation. The teacher's role here is to help students create categories and locations by questioning and encouraging them rather than by doing the organizing for them.

To help students understand left–right and top–bottom relationships, I use tic-tac-toe with individuals and with whole classes. When I do the tic-tac-toe activity with a group, I demonstrate and each student draws his or her own tic-tac-toe grid. Here's how the process worked with Rob, an 8th grader.

Rob: Recognizing Relationships with Tic-Tac-Toe

I pointed to the three top boxes on Rob's tic-tac-toe grid and asked, "How are these three boxes alike? Where are they in relationship to the other boxes?"

"At the top," Rob said.

"Put a *T* in each top box," I directed him. Then I pointed to the bottom three boxes. "Where are these boxes?"

"At the bottom." He put a *B* in each box.

I pointed to the three boxes in the middle row. "And these?"

"In the middle." Rob put an *M* in each box.

I then drew another tic-tac-toe grid and pointed to the three boxes on the left, right, and middle. He wrote *L*, *R*, and *M* in the appropriate boxes. Then I drew a third tic-tac-toe grid and pointed to the top left box. "Everything we know is in relationship to something else," I said. "The secret to learning is finding relationships. Where is this box?"

"On the top," Rob answered.

As I pointed to the three boxes on the top row, I said, "It is one of these," and then I pointed to the three boxes on the left and said, "and one of these."

"It's top and left," Rob said, putting *TL* in the box.

To emphasize the relationship, I pointed to the top and left rows again and repeated, "It is one of these and one of these, but it is the only one that is top and left."

When I work with a whole class, students identify locations, including the middle middle box in the middle vertical column and the middle horizontal row. (See Figure 6.2 for a completed grid.) Then the students play tic-tac-toe and name each location. For example, one student says, "I put my *X* in top left," and another says, "I put my *O* in bottom right."

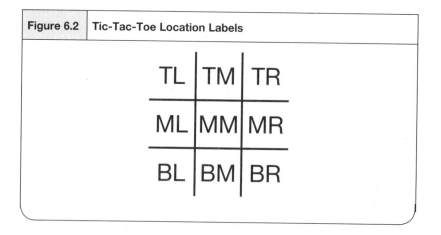

Figure 6.2 | **Tic-Tac-Toe Location Labels**

TL	TM	TR
ML	MM	MR
BL	BM	BR

By naming locations, students have to consciously think about where they are placing their marks. This slows down the game and raises awareness of spatial locations. Using the tower instrument described in Chapter 1 is another effective way to help students master left–right and top–bottom relationships.

Chuck: Left and Right Finally Stuck

One day a special education physical therapy teacher stopped me in the hall and asked, "What have you been doing with Chuck? We have tried for four years to teach him his left and right. Whatever you did with him stuck. He knows it now." Chuck, a 4th grader, and I had worked with tic-tac-toe and the tower. These activities helped him develop the cognitive structure of spatial orientation.

Chuck learned to identify spatial relationships by comparing where he was and where objects and places were in relationship to each other and to him. To do this, he became reflectively aware of what his senses were telling him. Chuck was able to visualize and mentally manipulate the information and then process it by comparing and classifying what he saw and where he was in relation to prior knowledge and experience. By developing his cognitive structures, he also developed his ability to learn, create, and change.

To promote this kind of development when I'm working with a large group, I use a game I call Rotate, which focuses on making "mental maps." When playing, we start with a tic-tac-toe grid and put a dot in any one of the boxes. Then students close their eyes and make mental maps by picturing where the dot would be if they rotated the paper a quarter-turn clockwise without physically moving the paper or their bodies. This is a simple but powerful exercise that helps students visualize and move information around in their minds. For some, it is very difficult. They experiment by mentally rotating the grid with the dot clockwise two, three, and four one-quarter turns. As they become more proficient at making mental maps, they experiment with two or more dots on a grid, as shown in Figure 6.3.

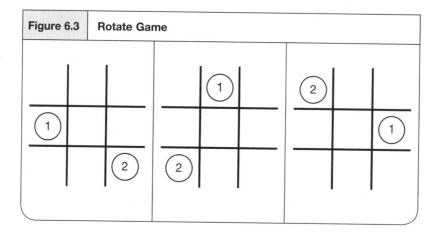

| Figure 6.3 | Rotate Game |

Before students can plan, solve problems, think abstractly, and comprehend what they read and hear, they must be able to mentally represent ideas, persons, places, and things in relation to each other. Simple visualization exercises can help students develop this aspect of spatial orientation.

We can also help students by naming specific locations when giving directions, for example, "Put the book on the bottom-left shelf." Too often, teachers give vague directions, and students become confused. The curriculum is filled with opportunities to help students develop an understanding of how location affects their lives. Here's how Kelly, a kindergarten teacher, helped students develop spatial orientation development during everyday instruction.

Kelly's Puzzlemania

At the beginning of a lesson, Kelly gathered her students around a picture or set of instructional materials and asked, "What do you notice?" Immediately, hands went up. Students spontaneously wanted to get up and point to items of interest. Instead, Kelly had them identify the location of an item before describing what they noticed. At first they resisted and felt frustrated. Gradually, they became more comfortable and would make comments like this: "In the middle left of the picture, I noticed a green tree." They would then describe not just what they saw but also what they noticed about the particular item in relationship to other items: "I noticed that this tree is smaller than the one on the middle right and that they both have shadows under them."

With this simple activity, Kelly helped students to become more reflectively aware of what their senses were telling them and to develop their language skills. As students get older, they need to know how to identify locations on Earth using standardized, worldwide reference systems such as latitude and longitude, cardinal directions, and Global Positioning Systems.

Distance. We use distance to define intervals of separation between and among objects. In physical space, distance is the size of the gap between two objects or persons. We use lines, words, symbols, illustrations, graphics, and diagrams to represent distance. Artists use various techniques to represent distance on a flat surface. In school, representational distance is embedded in every subject area. For example, in math, students learn about measuring length. In reading and writing, the distance between letters and words makes them legible. When students learn to write an *A* or a *5*, they need to know how far to go with a line before changing direction to make the shape of the letter or number. In social studies, students must be able to understand how maps depict distance.

Through visualization, we use mental images to represent and manipulate distance. We use cultural, personal, and emotional norms to define virtual distance such as degrees of kinship or proximity when speaking to someone. Emotional distance refers to closeness of sentimental ties.

Margaret: A Frustrated Social Studies Teacher

Margaret taught 7th grade social studies and was very frustrated with her class because so many of them could not seem to understand drawing maps to scale. She explained, modeled, and provided worksheets for practice, but the students were just not getting it.

When she told me about this situation, I asked her how she might explain scale in terms of spatial orientation. Even though she had participated in training focused on cognitive structures, she hadn't made the connection with content she was teaching in class. She said that she had explained how to measure the distances and use scale to draw a map. Then she paused and said, "You know, that's when I should ask them what they noticed. They need to focus on what changes and what stays the same when the map is smaller, how they would classify the information on the map, and where they would put everything in relationship to other things. Now I get it!"

Margaret's situation is typical. Teachers can work very hard. Students can complete assignments and even pass a test on the information by using imitation and memorization. However, before they can really learn, create, and change, they need to develop cognitive structures such as spatial orientation.

Direction. Direction identifies orientation toward a point of reference in both three-dimensional and two-dimensional space. North, south, east, and west–the cardinal directions—are external points of reference that are the same, regardless of what direction a person is facing.

Students need to understand the directional relationships represented on a two-dimensional map, on a globe, and in real life. Sometimes teachers unintentionally confuse students by pointing to a wall map and saying, "Now remember, east is right and west is left." I remember as a child thinking north was up, so going uphill was north. You may even know adults who get mixed up with cardinal directions. When asking or giving directions they say, "Don't tell me that east-west stuff, just tell me what's on the corner and whether I go left or right!"

Left and right are directional terms primarily used in relationship to which way a person is facing. Because young students often get mixed up with left and right directions, I do a simple turning activity to help them understand that left and right turn with them. I begin by asking students to stand, raise their right hands, and turn one quarter-turn to their left. Then I ask which hand is up. Everyone answers, "Right." I ask them to keep the same hand raised and turn another quarter turn, and I repeat the question: "Which hand is up?" Again, they answer, "Right!" We do this for two more turns. When they face me with their right hands raised, I raise my left hand and ask them which hand I have up. In every group (even among adults), some say I have my right hand up.

When I ask students to share what they noticed, they make the following types of comments: "I noticed my left hand turned when I turned, even when I had my right hand up"; "Everything on my right turned—my ear, my eye, my foot"; "If I raise my right hand and turn left, my right hand is still on my right side"; and "Your right is always on your right no matter where you go." With younger students, I repeat the activity using the left hand. Students may be able to name their right and left hands but not use that information when giving or following directions. When students confuse right and left, everything is confusing and they don't know why.

Orientation in space anchors people, places, and things in relationship to each other. To write letters and numbers, students need to know where to start and which direction to go on a two-dimensional surface. Straight lines are directional— vertical, horizontal, or diagonal. To help students connect these terms with direction, I have them say the word with a descriptor: "Horizontal, from left to right," "Vertical, up and down," or

"Diagonal, slanted from right to left," for example. Curved lines can go in any direction. Our reading, writing, and numbering systems are based on left–right and top–bottom relationships. Students who write their letters backward or who have been diagnosed with dyslexia need to develop spatial cognitive structures, especially left–right relationships. Figure 6.4 shows examples of letters and numbers that students often find confusing because they have not noticed the relation of the spatial elements. To help students develop spatial structures, I write a set of letters, like *bdpq* and ask them what they notice. It is important for them to compare and contrast each element of a letter in terms of location, distance, and direction.

Figure 6.4	Letters and Numbers That Are Easily Confused		
b d p q	r h u n	s z E 3	6 9 2 7

Students who do not have stable left–right orientation also have difficulty writing cursive letters (especially lowercase *f* and *q*) and writing numbers. Instead of just teaching students how to write their letters or numbers through drill and practice, it is important to take the time to make sure they have spatial orientation.

Strategies such as putting an *L* on the left hand and an *R* on the right tend to make students dependent on the cue. Using the pointer finger and thumb to make an *L* to identify the left hand works only if students already have stable directionality, otherwise they don't know the *L* is backward when they use their right finger and thumb to make an *L*. Sayings such as "I write with my right" may be helpful for right-handers but not for left-handers. Not having well-developed spatial orientation affects many different aspects of life and can be a major source of confusion and frustration. Here's a good example.

Donny: Math and Spatial Orientation

Donny was a 30-year-old college student who had completed all but one of his degree requirements. He explained to me that although he had taken Algebra five times, had been tutored, and had put in hours of study time, he just couldn't complete the work and pass the course. He said he was always slow in school and had been diagnosed with learning disabilities but was very good in language arts and had even published two children's books. Still, math was something he just couldn't seem to get.

I did a quick assessment of Donny's basic cognitive structures. He enjoyed demonstrating his ability to classify, memorize, and comprehend what he read. However, when I asked him to identify left and right and cardinal directions, he stumbled. With some embarrassment, Donny admitted that yes, directions were a big problem. "I can't seem to keep a job," he told me. "It's really hard for me to find my way for an interview. If I get a job, I end up getting fired because I'm always late. I just get lost."

I told Donny I suspected that his struggles with math and his difficulty with directions were probably related. He was skeptical but agreed to try out an activity I had in mind. I gave him a paper with an *X* and four shapes drawn on it (see Figure 6.5). Then, I asked Donny to picture himself standing on the *X* facing the circle and then tell me what was on his left. He could not do this.

Figure 6.5	A Spatial Orientation Exercise

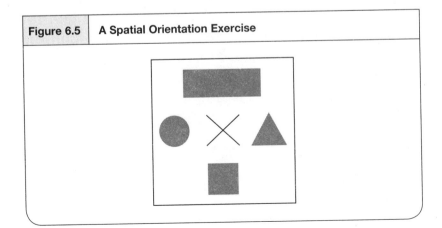

Next, we put objects on the floor so he could face one and touch those to his right and left before trying to visualize the location of objects. We also worked with the tower. Going from physical objects to abstract representation of objects in relationship to his body was very challenging for him. He began making mental maps to abstractly represent sensory information. When he realized his capabilities, he said, "Wow! I feel like I am using parts of my brain I never used before!"

I worked with Donny several more times to strengthen his spatial orientation and review basic math concepts. He found that they made more sense because he could finally visualize elements of equations in relation to one another. He became more relaxed and confident as he grasped what math problems stood for and used his logical reasoning to solve them. About six months later, Donny called to let me know he had passed Algebra, received his degree, and gotten the job he'd wanted.

Perspective. This requires using a specific point of reference to identify distance and position within a personal field of vision. Perspective includes material, representational, abstract, and virtual space based on (1) who is seeing, (2) what is being seen, and (3) where the person is focusing (focal point). These three elements are related to perception, purpose, opinion, and point of view and can be affected by physical, mental, emotional, personal, and political factors. Each person uses values, beliefs, feelings, knowledge, skills, and experience to filter what is seen and how it is seen. For many years, I used a Disney art education film in which four artists with very different styles painted pictures of the same gnarled oak tree. One artist painted a near-photographic image; one blended impressionistic light and color; one used abstract, cubistic shapes; and one made it a cartoon character. It was a powerful illustration of individual perspective.

From a psychological point of view, perspective is the ability to put oneself in another's place and see and feel what that person sees and feels. Sometimes teachers scold a child by saying, "How would you feel if somebody did that to you?" If the child doesn't have perspective, the words are meaningless. We can help students develop perspective by doing some simple activities.

Joan: Visualizing Different Perspectives

Joan, a 2nd grader, was often inconsiderate of others. To help her become aware of the need for perspective, we sat across from each other at a small square table. I placed a cup with a handle in front of her and asked, "What do you notice?"

"It has a handle," she responded.

"Where is the handle?"

Joan pointed. "Right here."

"Where is 'right here'?" I asked.

"On the side of the cup."

"Which side?"

Joan looked at her hands and then raised her right hand. "On the right side."

"OK. Now I'm going to turn the cup around." I turned the cup so the handle was to Joan's left. "If you were sitting where I am sitting, which side of the cup would the handle be on?"

Joan got up and moved beside me. "On the right." Then she went back to her place.

I turned the cup one quarter-turn clockwise. "Where would the handle be if you were sitting there?" I asked, pointing to the empty side of the table on my right.

Joan started to get up and go around the table.

"Wait," I said. "See if you can picture it in your mind without moving."

Joan looked puzzled, closed her eyes, and moved her hands as if turning the cup. Then, with her eyes partly open, she turned her body as if looking from the other position. "Now I see it! It would be on the left."

"Great! Let's do it again," I responded. "This time, see if you can do it all in your mind without moving your body." I moved the handle in front of her. "If you were sitting over there," I said, pointing to the side of the table on my left, "where would the handle be?"

Joan rolled her eyes and looked at the side of the table as if moving her body in her mind. She thought a few seconds, smiled, and said confidently, "On the left." This was a major step for Joan. After that, she practiced considering specific playground and classroom incidents from different children's points of view.

In my art classes, I challenged students to become reflectively aware of all aspects of spatial relationships. To help them see things in relation to their eye level, for example, I had them stand in front of a tall empty bookshelf until they noticed what their eyes were telling them about how much of each shelf was visible (see Figure 6.6).

| Figure 6.6 | A Spatial Orientation Exercise in Perspective |

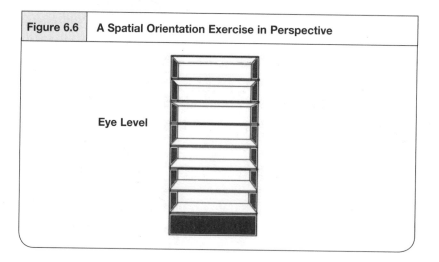

Eye Level

We studied long halls by using an index card with a small rectangular hole to observe how walls, doors, windows, lights, and floor tiles looked in relation to the edges of the hole. Students practiced using different frames and strategies to create the illusion of depth. They also enjoyed drawing buildings and geometric forms from various perspectives. When students viewed railroad tracks with rails that appeared to converge in the distance, they sometimes had difficulty understanding how the rails could be the same distance apart and yet seem to touch each other.

In parent and teacher training sessions, I did the same kinds of activities. For many adults, it was the first time they became aware of the spatial relationships they took for granted in everyday life. One parent shared her experience after becoming more spatially aware. "Last night I went to the opera," she explained. "When I walked into the theater, everything became so three-dimensional—the fixtures, stage, stairs, rows of seats, just everything. I could not believe how exciting it was!" Another said, "I really have to catch myself when I'm driving now, because I see my windshield as a frame and notice where things outside are in relation to the edges of my windshield. It's like, *wow!*" He just shook his head and smiled at his new awareness of spatial relationships.

Perspective is embedded in every content area in school. All curricula—including textbooks, activities, lesson plans, and assignments—are selected and organized according to someone's perspective. In language arts, students need to be aware that the writer describes characters and events from his or her point of view. In science, perspective influences observations, experiments, data collection, analysis, and research. In social studies, world events, places, cultures, and characters are recorded according to the perspectives of those reporting. In mathematics, especially geometry and statistics, point of view affects outcomes. In the arts and physical education, perspective permeates all aspects of performance and representation.

Suggestions for Practice

1. *Ask students, "What do you notice?" and "What would it look like from a different point of view?"* Encourage students to give details of size, shape, color, texture, and so on.

2. *Encourage students to describe where an object is in relationship to other objects,* for example, "The book is on the table

near the edge in front of me. A paper is under the book, and a pencil is to the left." This can be great fun, especially when students begin describing objects from different perspectives.

3. *Encourage students to notice when they need spatial orientation in every school subject.* Make a game of identifying and describing spatial relationships.

4. *Give directions and instructions in terms of physical spatial relationships.* Consciously use spatial words such as *left, right, top, bottom, north, south, east, west, horizontal, vertical, diagonal, over, under, between,* and *behind.* Be sure students have a clear understanding of these terms and how to use them.

5. *Play the Verbal Directions game* with equal, matching sets of blocks and a visual barrier between the two participants. One person gives directions on how to build something while building it; the other person follows the directions without asking questions. After completing the building activity, they take down the barrier and compare the results. A variation of this activity uses paper and pencil with two students sitting back to back and one giving directions to the other about what to draw, using only directional terms and without naming or describing the object, shape, or design.

6. *Encourage students to draw what they see,* to represent three-dimensional objects on a two-dimensional surface. When they build something with blocks, Legos, pattern blocks, clay, or other objects, encourage them to draw what they have built. This helps them notice where parts are in relationship to each other and to the whole.

7. *Encourage students to draw floor plans* or diagrams of their house, room, classroom, school, or playground. Encourage them to mentally walk through the area as they draw it, using only directional terms and without naming or describing the object, shape, or design.

8. *Encourage students to visualize and plan how to go from one place to another.* When traveling, mentally picture and describe direction, distance, location, and perspective.

9. *Encourage students to become aware of how they can mentally manipulate and graphically represent abstract information* using diagrams, matrices, mind maps, and so on.

10. *Help students understand virtual space* in terms of computer simulations, personal space, and family relationships.

11. *Help students understand how they can use awareness of location to organize their physical world.* Discuss how having order reduces stress and confusion. Spatial orientation helps students identify and use specific places for specific things so they can easily find them when needed. Encourage students to get and return objects from assigned locations, and to notice where the location is in relationship to other locations.

12. *Play tic-tac-toe with students.* Have students name the location of each tic-tac-toe mark in terms of left–right and top–bottom relationships. This simple game is also useful in helping students plan ahead by visualizing how their marks will affect their partner's potential marks.

13. *Play Rotate* using points on a tic-tac-toe grid. Place one dot, then ask where it would be if you rotated the paper clockwise one quarter-turn, and so on. Do this activity using two or more dots at the same time.

14. *Encourage students to use a map, globe, compass, and GPS device to locate places.* These tools help them identify spatial relationships.

15. *Encourage students to measure distance and length* with various units. Ask, "How far is it from home to school in miles, feet, inches, and meters? How far is it if you walk or ride your bike?"

16. *Encourage students to notice their perspectives* and to mentally put themselves in another's place and try to see something as that person sees it. Encourage students to draw objects from different points of view, for example, viewing something from the back, closer or farther away, looking down from the top (bird's-eye view), or looking up from an ant's perspective.

7

Temporal Orientation

Jennifer came running in to see her 6th grade social studies teacher. Gasping for breath, she said excitedly, "I found the pattern in social studies!" Ms. Thomas mirrored her student's excitement and asked, "You did? What did you find?" Jennifer blurted out, "It's the time line! The time line shows how all the things that happened fit together!" Ms. Thomas clapped and celebrated with Jennifer, recognizing that this student's ability to identify patterns and relationships by classifying and organizing data into related time units was a sign of developing temporal orientation.

Temporal Orientation Defined

Temporal orientation is a cognitive structure for processing information by comparing events in relationship to *when* they occur. This involves the critical skill of telling time and much more. It is essential for planning, organizing, communicating, and record keeping, and it enhances the study of literature, science, social studies, math, arts, music, and physical education.

When students have temporal orientation, they can *make connections* by comparing data with other knowledge and experience;

find patterns and relationships by classifying and organizing data into related units; *formulate rules* by identifying predictable patterns that accelerate processing; and *abstract generalizable principles* by transferring and applying information in many different applications.

When we tell students to "think before you act," we assume they have temporal orientation. This cognitive structure also helps students delay gratification and control impulses by inserting an interval of time between stimulus and response. This gives them time to reflect and process information: to consider cause–effect relationships and possible outcomes and then make a decision about what to do next.

Lots of us complain about not having enough time. Temporal orientation helps us plan and organize more effectively. Like all cognitive structures, it is influenced by values, beliefs, and feelings. For example, have you ever noticed that people often use the same terms when talking about time that they use when talking about money? Both are things we *spend, use, invest, waste, give, take, manage,* and so on. In other contexts, we talk about *filling time, passing time, killing time,* or *having time on our hands.* All of these reflect our perception that time is a thing we can control. Of course, the amount of time in each day remains the same; all we can control is our use of it.

Helping Students Develop Temporal Orientation

It is useful to group time into three interdependent categories: *traits or characteristics of time, types or phases of time,* and *motion or movement of time* (see Figure 7.1). Each of these categories is related to physical, representational, abstract, or virtual space (see Chapter 6). That is, we can use temporal orientation in relation to our physical and sensory world. We can represent it through drawings, diagrams, words, music, and other symbol systems. We can mentally visualize and manipulate temporal information

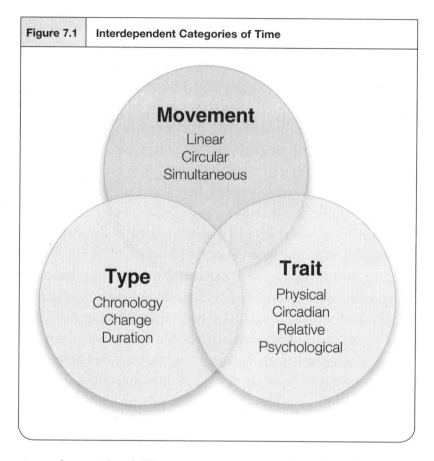

Figure 7.1 | **Interdependent Categories of Time**

at an abstract level. We can project virtual time through simulations and cultural or generational relationships.

The categories of temporal orientation—traits, types, and movement—are embedded in culture and environment, which provide their context for development, evidence of use, and mode of expression. Students in modern, industrialized cultures with clocks on nearly every wall and on most electronic devices perceive time differently from students in cultures where timepieces are rare. Our understanding of news events, literature, arts, sciences, languages, economics, politics, religions, mathematics, technology, customs, every form of communication, and social interaction is dependent on their location and time period. Because of societal changes in family structures, disconnection among family members, disruptions caused by war and other disasters, and the fast pace of living, many students in today's classrooms are disoriented in time and space. This disorientation affects their ability to learn because they are not making connections when teachers present information. What's more, students who have irregular or nonexistent routines at home tend to be insecure and easily distracted when faced with a heavily structured school day.

Traits of Time

It can be helpful to think of time in terms of its various traits: *physical, circadian, relative,* and *psychological.*

Physical. This time trait involves physical things, such as persons, objects, and events that can be perceived by the senses. Students need to know how to use standard devices such as a clock and calendar for measuring time. They also need to understand how time and space are interconnected. We use phrases such as "when it took place" or "I was there when it happened." When and where something happens are key indicators for organizing information.

Circadian. Saying that time is circadian describes how it is governed by our natural body rhythms, an internal clock based on experience and conscious development that regulates cycles of the body, such as activity and rest. Global travel and working swing shifts can interrupt these cycles. For students, interruptions come from irregular or inadequate sleeping or eating habits that leave them unable to focus and function effectively in the classroom.

Relative. In simple terms, measurements of time vary according to relative motion. Einstein's theories of relativity changed our understanding of time and space. His ability to think beyond the constraints of conventional scientific beliefs, theories, and practices enabled him to explain complex issues of time-space that go beyond the scope of this book. Everything we do is in relationship to something else, so we are affected by relativity whether or not we are aware of it.

Psychological. Time is linked to personal perception and depends on prior knowledge, experiences, attitudes, values, beliefs, emotions, health, preparation, and planning. How we perceive time is embedded in culture. For example, some cultures value speed and the efficient use of time; others value reflection and a slower, more relaxed pace of activities.

Three Types of Time

Types or phases of time identify periods and include *chronology, change,* and *duration.*

Chronology. Also known as *tense,* chronology identifies what is past, present, and future. Languages usually have various verb forms to express tense. Although it is important to be present and live in the now, it is also important to understand how the past has influenced the present and how the present influences the future. I remember the struggle I went through to learn to be present, that is, to keep my mind where my body is. It is easy to miss current happenings if we are worrying about the past or future. Most children live in the now, with little awareness of chronology. Temporal orientation helps us appreciate the past, benefit from the present, and prepare for the future. Teachers can help students develop a sense of belonging by grounding them in their personal family history and their collective cultural history.

Change. As a type of temporal orientation, change modifies what happens over time. As seconds tick by, we change physically, cognitively, and emotionally. Change can be gradual or sudden, orderly or chaotic, but something is always different. It is related to the other time categories; for example, the type of change can happen in the past, present, or future and be short or long term; the motion of change can be simultaneous, circular, or linear; the traits or characteristics of change can be physical, circadian, relative, or psychological. All change is embedded in culture and environment, which can provide a secure foundation for ongoing adaptation or form a barrier of tradition for resistance.

Duration. This designates the length of intervals from one point in time to another. Many students have difficulty planning and completing tasks on time because they are unaware of duration. For everyday use, duration is measured in seconds, minutes, hours, days, weeks, months, and years. These periods of duration provide a frame of reference to compare and process information in relation to time. Here is an example of how a 1st grade teacher helped a student understand duration.

Annie: "Is It Time Yet?"

Annie was six years old. In class, she frequently asked, "Is it time to go home?"

One day, during independent research time, her teacher, Mr. Todd, pointed to a large clock and asked Annie how long it would take for the big hand to go from 3 to 4. She looked totally confused. He led her to a learning station with 5 one-minute sand timers. Mr. Todd asked Annie to notice the red second hand on the clock. He told her to turn one of the timers over when the red second hand was on 12 and then watch how long it took for the sand to run through the timer.

In one minute, Annie happily reported the bottle was empty when the red hand came back to 12. Mr. Todd explained that she just saw how long a minute was. He then asked her how many timers it would take for the long minute hand on the clock to go from 5 to 6. When the long hand was on 5, Annie inverted one sand timer. She repeated this, intently observing both the flow of sand and the clock. When the long hand was on 6, she told Mr. Todd it took all five timers. He explained that's how long five minutes lasted.

Then he asked how many timers it would take for the long hand to go from 7 to 8. Annie said she didn't know but eagerly set up her work area to find out. About 20 minutes later, Annie reported, "It takes five sand timers for the long hand to go from each number to the next! That's five minutes for each one, right?" She then held up her tablet where she had drawn the sand timers and put a mark each time one emptied. "Each one ran out four times. I counted 20 marks, so that must be 20 minutes, right?" Through her own research, Annie developed a sense of duration.

Instead of just telling Annie how to count by fives and memorize positions on the clock, her teacher showed her how to use her senses to collect and analyze data by comparing one bit of information (the flow of sand) with another piece of information (the movement of clock hands). Mr. Todd encouraged her to reflect on what she observed by questioning her and providing the opportunity for her to experiment on her own. By doing this, she began to understand duration and develop temporal orientation. As students become more effective using this cognitive structure, they can increase their ability to use time to learn, create, and change.

Movement of Time

Movement as a category of time encompasses *linear, circular,* and *simultaneous movement.* Despite the time-travel dreams of science fiction, time is irreversible. Actions, thoughts, and events can be repeated, but they are in relation to a different set of circumstances at a different time. As much as we would like to see into the future, we still have to depend on the predictability of previous patterns. Movement includes direction and rate of speed.

Linear movement. Also know as *sequential motion,* the linear movement of time describes what comes first, second, third, and so on, in terms of before and after relationships. Many students I work with have difficulty doing tasks and assignments that require sequencing because they have not developed this kind of temporal orientation. Although they can read a clock, they have not grasped that time is a way of comparing and sequencing information; instead, it is just one of many disconnected pieces of information they have memorized.

When presented with an unfamiliar task, these students are often confused about where to start and how to systematically proceed step by step. Scheduling provides predictability and order to a sequence of events; however, students need a balance between structured and unstructured time so they can learn to organize their own time. Students who grow up with no structured time have serious difficulties adapting to the constraints of schedules and planning a sequence of tasks.

Circular movement. This describes how the repetition of events over time establishes a rhythmic pattern for predictability and comparison. The circular movement of time can also spiral in expanding cycles. For example, trees that cycle through seasons are also growing larger. Scientists and engineers repeat experiments and expand on previous findings in a spiraling extension of research.

Simultaneous movement. This describes what happens in different locations at the same time. It is sometimes difficult for students to understand how so many events can be going on at any given moment. Stories and movies often use synchronized time to show what is happening in different places at the same time. History documents simultaneous worldwide events in specific time periods. Technology makes it possible to have live simulcasts of news events as they are happening. We can simultaneously process multiple bits of information. Although sophisticated computers can process enormous amounts of data quickly, most microprocessing systems use rapid linear sequences in cyclic patterns. Technical engineers are attempting to emulate the simultaneous processing capabilities of the human mind.

Learning to Tell (and Understand) Time

When students develop temporal orientation, they can organize events, activities, and information by comparing them with each other and to a specific reference point in time. Although temporal orientation means more than just reading the numbers on a clock, telling and understanding time are a necessary skills. Over the years, I worked with many middle school students who could read a digital watch but not a clock face. They were often late for class, did not turn work in on time, and could not organize and plan how to complete a task within a given time frame. These students also had difficulties with social studies because they did not understand the relationships of past, present, and future. In science and math, they had difficulty sequencing steps in an experiment or operation. In literature, they could not reference a time period to understand the context of a story. In language arts (reading and writing), they often mixed up the tenses of the verbs. They also had difficulty with spelling and writing events in chronological order. Developing temporal orientation equips students to organize and connect bits of information in relationship to each other and to standardized units of time.

Kim, a 2nd grader, helped me teach students to tell time on a face clock. She explained how confusing it was to look at different clocks because she couldn't tell which hand pointed to hours or minutes. Following Kim's instructions, I made a cardboard clock face with numbers in a small circle and dots in a larger concentric circle (see Figure 7.2). Every fifth dot was enlarged to identify five-minute intervals. The hour hand was short and reached only far enough to touch the numbers. The minute hand was long and narrow and reached far enough to touch the dots. The hands were attached with a brad and moved easily.

When using this clock, instead of explaining it, I give it to students and ask, "What do you see?" After they respond, I ask, "What do you notice?"

These are two different questions. The first is asking for sensory input, that is, what students see with their eyes. The second is asking for interpretation—what they see with their minds. This may sound very simple, but it is a powerful affirmation of the

Figure 7.2	Kim's Clock

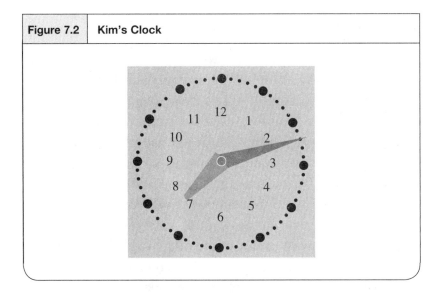

students' ability to gather information and construct meaning. "What do you see?" has a right-or-wrong, measurable response. "What do you notice?" does not have a right or wrong answer and activates an investigative approach to gathering data. It also stimulates reflective awareness and visualization, which are needed to develop cognitive structures. When students realize that they can use their cognitive structures to make connections, find patterns and relationships, generate rules to predict outcomes, and abstract generalizable principles that apply to many different situations, they develop metability.

Jim: Hands-On Practice Telling Time

Here is an example of how I used Kim's clock with Jim, a 4th grader who was confused about telling time. I set Kim's clock on the table and asked Jim what he saw. "A clock," he replied. When I asked him what else, he insisted, "Just a clock!"

Then I asked Jim what he *noticed* about the clock. "There's some numbers and dots," he replied.

When I prompted him to tell me what else he noticed, he said, "There are some cardboard hands." When I asked what he noticed about the hands, he said, "There are two of them. One is long and one is short. They're purple."

Then I asked Jim what he saw when he looked at the numbers. "They go from 1 to 12," he said. I asked what he noticed about them. "They're in a circle. Oh! And they are evenly spaced," he added. When I asked Jim what he noticed about the dots, he said, "They're in a bigger circle; some are big and some are small." Then I asked how many dots there were. Jim didn't know, so he counted them and discovered there were 60. With more prompting, Jim noticed that the short hand reached only to the numbers and the long hand touched the dots.

I asked what direction the numbers were going. "That way," Jim said, pointing clockwise around the circle. When I asked him if clock numbers always go that way, he looked around the room and noticed the clock on the wall and the clock on my desk. "They do on those clocks."

"When we start at the top of the circle and move to the right, we call that *clockwise*," I explained.

Learning how to gather sensory data is the first step of effective cognitive processing. Students who input superficial sensory data experience confusion and frustration. In class, Jim rarely noticed details and their relationships to each other. He did not read directions on worksheets; he just started doing them and made mistakes. Before we talked about using a clock to tell time, Jim had to gather and reflect on relevant sensory data. Only then was he ready to make connections and see patterns and relationships.

I explained to Jim that the numbers stand for hours. "The little hand only talks to numbers. The little hand always talks first," I said. Jim moved the short hand around. "The dots stand for minutes," I noted. "The long hand only talks to minutes. Point to the dots and count them again. Say the big dots real loud."

I showed Jim where to start; then he pointed and began counting each dot, emphasizing the larger dots ("One, two, three, four, *five,* six, seven . . ."). When he reached 20, I asked Jim what he noticed. "Wait a minute!" He pointed to the large dots and counted by fives: "Five, 10, 15, 20 . . ."

"OK. Let's see how all this fits together." I moved the short hand to the 5 and the long hand to a large dot by the 7. Jim watched closely. "The little hand talks first. To read the time, you would say 'Five' and then count dots to see what the long hand is saying."

Jim counted by ones and said, "Thirty-five."

"So the time is 5:35." Then I explained how we write time with the hour first, a colon, and then the minutes. "OK, let's try another time," I said, moving the short hand to the 7 and the long hand to a dot by the 3. "What do you know for sure?" I asked.

"The little hand talks first, and it is talking to the 7," Jim said. I asked him to write that, and he wrote a 7 with a colon after it. "The long hand is talking to this dot right here," he went on, pointing. "Let me see." He paused to think and then counted the dots up to 15. "So I write that here." He wrote 15 after the colon. "So it's 7:15!"

"You did it! Let's try another."

Jim practiced moving the clock hands and writing times. Next I asked him to write a time first and then move the hands. Each time he wrote a time, he read it aloud, always reading hour before minutes. When he put the short hand on 8 and the long hand on 12, I explained the term *o'clock,* saying, "We write 8:00 to start a new hour." We reviewed the names of hours, such as 2:00 and 5:00. I also explained how to write minutes less than 10 by using a zero after the colon, such as 9:05 and 11:07. Jim caught on quickly.

In telling the hour, students also get confused when the short hand is between numbers. To help Jim understand this pattern, I put the short hand on 4 and slowly moved it from the 4 to the 5 while saying, "The short hour hand is talking to the 4, is talking to the 4, is talking to the 4. . . . " When the short hand touched

5, I said, "Now, it's talking to the 5." After a little practice, Jim started counting by fives and could easily tell times such as 5:48 or 3:27. He always read time saying the hour and then the minutes, instead of using terms such as *quarter after, quarter till,* and *half past.* Students need to learn one thing really well before hearing too many different ways to do something. Once Jim felt confident, I gave him a real clock. I again asked, "What do you see?" and "What do you notice?"

"When I twist the long hand all the way around, the little hand goes only one number," he commented. When I asked Jim why that was the case, he continued experimenting, moving the hands around. Then he pointed to the dots on the cardboard clock. "It takes 60 minutes to make one hour."

Jim constructed meaning for himself by noticing patterns. He saw the relationship between minutes and hours by comparing the movement and positions of the hands. The real clock face had four minute lines instead of dots between each number. Jim hesitated when he tried to read the clock. I asked him to set the hands on the cardboard clock to match the hands on the real clock. By comparing how they were alike and different, he quickly adapted to reading the real clock. In a matter of minutes, he was feeling competent about telling time. I then asked Jim to switch roles—he became the teacher and I was the student. As he taught me, he was delighted to clearly explain the process and patterns in his own words.

In addition to temporal orientation, Jim also used other cognitive structures, such as recognition, spatial orientation, classification, symbolic representation, and logical reasoning. All of these helped him develop his ability to learn, create, and change. We had one problem though: his teacher said Jim kept raising his hand to tell everyone the time.

This approach for learning time is simple and effective for students of all ages in a classroom setting. One teacher asked me why I didn't put small numbers by the dots so students could more easily read the minutes. I explained that it was more effective for students to construct time patterns using the symbols (dots or lines). Unfortunately, some primary-grade lessons on time do not put any emphasis on helping students see patterns and relationships; instead, they simply teach students to memorize the positions of clock hands for the hour and half hour. For example, at 2:00, the big hand is on 12 and the little one is on 2; at 2:30, the big hand is on 6 and the little hand is on 2.

Mandy, a 3rd grader, was so upset when she couldn't tell time that she took the watch her parents had given her, stomped on it, and threw it away. After using Kim's clock, she said excitedly, "I can't believe I learned to tell time in just five minutes!"

Suggestions for Practice

1. *Encourage students to notice time-keeping devices* that are visible and useful in daily life. Explain how they work and why they are used.

2. *Encourage students to experiment with different ways of measuring time.* Arrange for them to experiment with sand timers, sundials, water clocks, pendulums, and various kinds of mechanical and electronic timers. Find old clocks and watches that they can take apart and examine to explore how they work. Stimulate reflection by asking thought-provoking questions.

3. *Encourage students to notice the relationship between the clock and the calendar.* Help them learn the meaning of time-related words such as *second, minute, hour, day, week, month, year, seasons, decades,* and *centuries.*

4. *Practice using time to plan and schedule activities.* Model for students how they can use the calendar to make short-term and long-term plans. For example, have them mark holidays, birthdays, activities, assignments, and so on in a personal planner or on a large wall calendar.

5. *Model good time management to help students use time effectively for work and relaxation.* Encourage students to estimate how long it will take them to accomplish a task, such as completing a homework assignment, cleaning their room, or doing the dishes. Help them see how planning, effort, and effectiveness can give them more free time.

6. *Encourage students to notice how events relate to each other in terms of past, present, and future.* Encourage them to notice how words, especially verbs, express time using different tenses. Demonstrate by telling or writing a story (the same story) as if it happened in the past, is happening now, or will happen in the future.

7. *Spend time teaching students about their family history, culture, and traditions.* Help students create and illustrate a family tree to show how all their relatives are connected to each other over time from one generation to the next. Celebrate cultural events. Use photo albums to help students understand that they are here because of the lives of those who went before them and that what they do will affect future generations.

8. *Help students understand duration or time intervals.* Encourage students to experiment with various kinds of time-keeping devices for long and short periods of time to get a feel for duration. Help them become aware of varying lengths of intervals in regard to personal activities, schedules, seasons, movies, commercials on TV, music notation, and so on. Ask them to notice how long it takes to get from one place to another if they are walking, riding a bike, riding in a car, or flying in an airplane.

9. *Encourage students to notice sequences, series, and other ordered relationships.* Students can learn to organize activities into a step-by-step series of procedures. Help them notice the relationship between sequences and time.

10. *Encourage students to become aware of recurring cycles, such as seasons, events, and behaviors.* Help them understand that the repeated events and behaviors may be the same but

they happen at different times. Encourage them to illustrate the seasons in relation to the calendar. They may also be interested in other kinds of seasons or recurring cycles, such as those related to sports, hunting, phases of the moon, market fluctuations, and life and death in nature.

11. *Encourage students to notice how many different events are going on in different places at the same time.* When students are listening to the news, watching TV or movies, or studying history or literature, help them become aware of when and where events are taking place and how they correlate with other events taking place at the same time. Create time lines and organize the relationships of specific events in different content areas. For example, in 1775, when the American Revolution was taking place, what was happening in science, literature, art, music, mathematics, governments in other countries, philosophy, and so on? In current events, document or illustrate occurrences around the world on one particular date.

12. *Use a simple clock face, as in Kim's clock, to help students learn to tell time.* Use the following steps:

- Place the clock in front of the child and ask: "What do you see?" "What do you notice?"
- Ask the child to count the dots.
- Explain that the short hand talks only to numbers. Numbers stand for hours.
- Explain that the long hand talks only to dots. Dots stand for minutes.
- Explain that the short hand always talks first.
- Practice reading and writing times, including minutes less than 10. Always do the hour first.
- Explain how to read the hour hand when it is between numbers.
- Give the child a real clock face and ask what he or she sees and notices.

- Ask the child to compare a real clock and a cardboard clock.
- Encourage the child to experiment with turning the hands and to notice the relationship of minutes and hours—once around with the long minute hand equals one hour.
- Practice reading and writing time using the real clock.
- Ask the child to be the teacher and explain how to teach someone else how to tell time.

8

Metaphorical Thinking

Every 40 minutes, art class started with a peaceful hush. Students knew the routine. They walked in, sat down, and closed their eyes to think "a beautiful thought" and get their imaginations working. After a few seconds, I would quietly ask, "Who would like to share their beautiful thought?" Most hands went up, and during the next few minutes, students eagerly shared their beautiful thoughts with me or with other students at their tables: "I was wondering what it would be like to be a fish and swim all day"; "I saw myself as a seed that was buried and then I started to grow and stretch out my leaves to catch the sun"; "When I held my new baby sister, she was like a living doll." This little activity, which I used with students in kindergarten through 8th grade, set a creative, reflective tone and provided focus for creative expression. (Because older students were sometimes self-conscious about sharing their beautiful thoughts aloud, I gave them the option of drawing or writing them instead.) For many of my students, art was an oasis, a welcome relief from their perceived desert of academic frustration and failure.

Students who are struggling are often creative, metaphorical thinkers who do not understand why their schoolwork is so difficult. They are usually unaware that their creative way of processing information is out of sync with the straightforward, logical expectations of the curriculum. As I worked with these students, they were surprised to learn that their metaphorical thinking was a precious asset.

Metaphorical Thinking Defined

Metaphorical thinking is a cognitive structure for making sense of information by comparing one thing to another using figurative language. As educators know, a metaphor is a word or phrase that describes one thing as if it is something else. Metaphors bring home meaning by emphasizing similarities and overlooking differences, and they often use forms of the verb "to be." For example, "The man is a workhorse!" "The leaves are dancing in the wind."

As a cognitive structure, metaphorical thinking is inferential and creative. It is a form of comparative thinking that equips students to generate fresh insights and understanding through unusual connections. For this reason, I include other familiar literary devices, such as simile, analogy, and personification in my definition of metaphorical thinking. Simile makes a comparison explicit by saying something is "like" something else: "This problem is like a mountain." Analogy compares one similar aspect of very different things and infers that a small resemblance implies further similarities: "Foot is to sock as hand is to glove." Personification represents a thing as if it were a person or had human characteristics: "The hungry flames of the brushfire devoured the parched fields."

Like other cognitive structures, metaphorical thinking can be used in every content area to develop metability. Language, both written and spoken, is peppered with metaphors. In English and language arts classes, students delight in becoming detectives, identifying where they notice metaphors and discussing the appropriateness of the imagery. They often enjoy coming up with their own metaphors that might be more colorful, humorous, or effective than the one used by an author. When students write their own stories, metaphors add personal depth of meaning to their words. When they do public speaking or presentations, metaphors add creativity and stimulate interest.

Although metaphor is most familiar to us as a literary device, it can play a role in other curriculum areas as well. In science, metaphors provide a useful way to help students understand unfamiliar ideas. In mathematics, a teacher might ask students to use metaphorical thinking and draw their understanding of an abstract concept. In social studies, various cultural and economic metaphors have become integrated into everyday usage—for example, daily reports on the stock exchanges' bull or bear markets. In physical education, a teacher might encourage students to run like the wind or do rabbit jumps. In the arts, metaphors permeate every form of creative expression.

The best way to generate metaphors is to be playfully creative. When we explain something to students, we can quickly check their understanding by asking, "What sense do you make of this?" or "What does this mean to you?" These questions are very different from asking, "What did I say?" or "What did you hear?" which asks students to use short-term memory to simply repeat the information. Inviting students to communicate their understanding relieves fear of getting the answer wrong and gives them the opportunity to construct meaning for themselves. Responses can be shared with small or large groups. Just a word of caution, though: Metaphors are useful because they make a point. They can outlive their usefulness if the comparisons are extended beyond the scope of the intended meaning. Helping students understand the appropriateness of metaphors will support effective learning.

Helping Students Integrate Metaphorical Thinking

It is challenging to help students integrate metaphorical thinking
—the creative language of poets, artists, and comedians—with
the logical thinking often valued in the classroom. This "integration difficulty" is fairly common among students whom classmates consider "weird"—students whose unusual questions or
explanations reveal them to be on a different wavelength. Bobby
was one of these students.

Bobby: "A Space Cadet"

Bobby's 7th grade teacher described him as a space cadet who
gave unexpected, incorrect responses to her questions. She also
complained, "He can't concentrate, talks all the time, goofs off, is
unmotivated, and doesn't do his work!"

Bobby's parents were concerned about his negative attitude
toward school. They took him for a physical exam and had him
tested for learning disabilities. Results were average in all areas.
When I started to work with Bobby to assess his cognitive structures, he was impulsive and didn't seem to understand how
to do the activities. He often responded to my questions with
nonverbal grunts or a shrug of the shoulders. My initial assessment revealed that Bobby's logical reasoning, spatial orientation, and temporal orientation were inefficient. He mixed up left
and right, and he was unsure of directions such as horizontal or
vertical and north, south, east, and west. He could not explain
the relationship between the clock and the calendar and had no
idea how many weeks were in a year or days were in a month.
He depended on recognition, guessing, and memorization when
doing school-related tasks. He was passive and took little or no
responsibility for his own learning.

About the only thing in school Bobby enjoyed was art class,
where he showed exceptional ability and creativity. When he was
drawing or painting, he could focus for hours and was always

happy to complete projects. He was focused and precise in his work, noticed details and relationships, and solved problems effectively. However, Bobby did not see any connection between what he did there and what was required in his academic classes, where he was disinterested, impulsive, and careless about his work.

During our interactions, Bobby enjoyed doing nonacademic, problem-solving activities, but the minute I gave him schoolwork, he reverted to well-practiced avoidance behaviors such as joking around, changing the subject, and complaining that he was tired. When he realized that I wanted him to complete a worksheet, for example, he scanned it quickly and superficially before beginning to do it incorrectly. He mumbled angrily, "Let's get it over with!"

When I questioned him about this approach, Bobby became argumentative and tried to justify his actions. What I saw was that he used intuitive, simultaneous thought patterns and had difficulty with logical, sequential thinking. When asked to explain his response to a problem, he would say, "I just know it. I don't know why." Instead of gathering sensory data, he used metaphorical thought patterns to represent things figuratively and creatively.

For example, Bobby and I worked with the tower, the assessment instrument described in Chapter 1 (see Figure 1.2, p. 19). It is made of six black square blocks, each drilled with nine holes, with all the holes fitted with a wooden peg. On each block, one peg is glued in place, and the other eight can be twisted in the holes. I placed the tower in front of Bobby and asked what he saw.

He looked at it with curiosity and said, "A tall building under construction."

"Tell me more," I said.

"Umm . . . I see an electricity thing," he said. "One of those tower things where wires hook up. Or it could be jail."

When I asked if he saw anything else, he said, "A parking garage."

Bobby did not give me any descriptive sensory data, such as color, size, shape, texture, number, or position. He used his imagination to metaphorically interpret what he saw. Creative students often use intuitive sensations to create meaning. These nonlinear, simultaneous forms of thinking make it possible for them to process information very rapidly and to make unpredictable connections—the kinds of "spacey" or "incorrect" answers that had irritated Bobby's teacher. Without reflective awareness and systematic processing, metaphorical thinking can be random and unproductive. *With* reflective awareness and visualization, however, metaphorical thinking becomes a powerful cognitive structure. The obstacle for Bobby was that he was unaware of how he thought. He just knew that schoolwork was hard and confusing.

I explained to Bobby what had happened during our discussion. "When I asked, 'What do you see?' you told me what you saw with your *mind,* not what you saw with your *eyes.*"

"Huh? What do you mean?" he responded.

I asked Bobby what color the tower's blocks were, and he answered, "Black." I asked him what shape the blocks were, and he said, "Square." When I asked him how many blocks there were, he counted them and said, "Six."

Then I asked Bobby what else he noticed, and he became very engaged, carefully examining the blocks. "There are nine sticks on each block," he said. "They are stacked up. The paint is shiny. The wood grain is all going the same way. The blocks are about an inch thick. They are all the same size. They are made of wood. There are shadows where the light is hitting. They are hard." He paused, tilting his head and still looking at the stack of blocks, totally focused. "They are on the table. They are in front of me. The pegs are all the same height." He picked up one block. "They can be moved. They are not very heavy."

"Wow! Look at what you just did!" I said. Bobby smiled, obviously enjoying himself. "Now, what did you do differently this time?" I asked. "Did you see all that stuff before?"

"Not really. Well, yeah, but I didn't pay any attention to it. I mean I didn't notice it, but it was just there," Bobby paused, thinking. "You know . . . I bet I do that with everything!"

"What do you mean?" I prompted.

"Like, miss a lot," he responded.

"What are you saying?" I asked.

"Well, like, the teacher tells us to do something, and I miss a lot of what she says, or something."

"Let me tell you what I think is happening, and you tell me if I'm right or not," I said.

"OK," Bobby replied, looking at me with skepticism.

"When you look at something, instead of seeing with your eyes, you see with your mind," I said. "You immediately see what it reminds you of rather than what you are actually seeing—just like you did here with the blocks. You said that you saw a parking garage, a jail. You *interpreted* what you saw rather than *describing* what you saw. I bet the same thing happens when you hear something in class. Instead of hearing the actual words, you hear what you think they are going to say."

Bobby became animated and said, "You're right! Then the teacher yells at me for not paying attention." He shook his head, smiling. "This is too weird!"

"Being able to think creatively in pictures is a real strength, a gift," I said. "It's called metaphorical thinking."

"Meta-what?" he asked.

"Metaphorical. A metaphor is a way of describing one thing as if it is something else. You just described the blocks as a building under construction. Or you might say something like, 'The story reflects your feelings.' The story is not a mirror, but you can compare it to a mirror because it copies or tells about how you feel." Bobby looked puzzled. "What did you understand by that?"

"Thinking in metaphors is good and it's bad," he said.

"Actually, it's the way poets, geniuses, and artists think," I said.

"But it's not the way teachers think!" Bobby said.

"Well, sometimes not," I smiled. "You just have to know for yourself when to use metaphorical thinking and when to use the kind of logical thinking you need for schoolwork and other things. You have to decide when to see with your eyes and when to see with your mind."

Before we began to work together, Bobby didn't know why he was always confused and schoolwork didn't make sense. Like so many other creative students, he was on a different wavelength. He explained that he would study for two hours for a test and still get an *F* on it. He did not realize that the way he input and processed information was very different from how it was presented. So when he took a test, he performed as if he had never seen the information because it was not what he had processed. Bobby demonstrated that he was perfectly capable of gathering sensory data with his eyes. When he was drawing, he noticed every little detail and how parts related to each other and to the whole. He hadn't thought of using that same capability in schoolwork. I explained that he needed to use both kinds of thinking, creative and logical, just as a bird needs two wings to fly. To help him understand the relationship between logic and creativity, I used a metaphor, knowing that he had been studying the body in biology.

"Think of creativity like the organs of the body," I said.

"You mean like the heart, lungs, liver, stomach, and stuff?" Bobby asked.

"Yes," I said. "The organs are soft, flexible, and absolutely essential for life."

"Yeah. You can't live without a heart!" Bobby responded.

"Right. The organs are like creativity and metaphorical thinking. The skeleton is a hard, flexible framework that supports the organs. Without a skeleton, organs would be a blob of tissues. The skeleton provides structure and support for the organs," I explained, while Bobby cocked his head and listened. "The skeleton needs the organs and tissues to move and function. The skeleton is like logical thinking. You need both to be complete. They are interdependent. Metaphorical and logical thinking are also interdependent." I paused. "Now, what sense did you make of that?"

Smiling, Bobby said, "I can do both—see with my mind and with my eyes." After a long pause, he sat up in the chair smiling broadly. "I can't wait to tell my mom!"

"What do you mean?" I asked.

"I can't wait to tell her that I'm not dumb and stupid," Bobby said. His eyes glistened with confidence and newly found respect for himself and his own capabilities. I encouraged him to use his "artist's eyes" to notice details, patterns, and relationships when he looked at "school stuff." He smiled at the thought of using his creativity to learn. He breathed a sigh of relief and said, "This could make schoolwork a whole lot easier!"

As we continued working with school-related activities, Bobby became more reflectively aware of how he gathered, processed, and expressed information. He saw how his ability to notice details combined with his metaphorical thinking could help him create meaning and learn more effectively.

Helping Students Apply Metaphorical Thinking

Students who are metaphorical thinkers need to understand the value and power of metaphors for comparing and making meaning. Metaphors evoke images that explain, inspire, interpret, and amuse. They are often permeated with emotions related to the images and are easily remembered. Metaphors add color and character to speech and writing. They make connections through comparisons, identify patterns and relationships, and enhance meaning through interpretive analysis. Because metaphorical thinkers bypass logic, they can make extraordinary intuitive leaps that might otherwise take years of research.

Creative students often express their understanding as a metaphor. We can use their responses to assess their comprehension, clarify misunderstandings, and encourage discussion. When we use metaphors to present lessons, we stimulate visualization. This helps students develop their ability to learn, create, and change. Our understanding, acceptance, appreciation, and encouragement of metaphorical thinking will make it much easier to access the capabilities of creative students. Bill is an example of how some students see things differently.

Bill: Seeing the Squares in the Hexagons

Bill was a 6th grader and a strong metaphorical thinker who studied for hours but did poorly on tests. He loved art class, where he demonstrated exceptional abilities in drawing, and he enjoyed playing his guitar. In academic classes, Bill did not input information the way it was presented. He creatively transformed and interpreted what he saw and heard. Once I gave Bill a paper with hexagons on it and asked what he saw.

Bill looked at the paper for a few seconds and said, "A bunch of squares."

"What makes a shape a square?" I asked, prompting him to explain.

"Four equal sides and four 90-degree angles," he responded.

"What do you see here?" I asked.

"Squares," he responded again.

"How many sides do you see?" I asked. "Count them."

Bill counted aloud, "One, two, three, four, five, six. But I still see squares."

"Help me understand," I prompted.

"It's like this," Bill said. "I can't really explain it, but I can show you." He picked up a pencil and drew three lines on one of the hexagons to form a cube (see Figure 8.1). "See. Like this. Oh, I guess it is more like a 3–D square or cube."

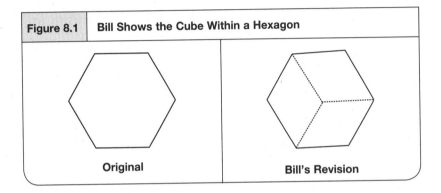

Figure 8.1	Bill Shows the Cube Within a Hexagon
Original	Bill's Revision

"Wow! What you see with your mind is different from what you see with your eyes," I explained.

"What does that mean?" he asked.

"I saw a hexagon," I said. "You saw a cube."

"Yeah, so?" Bill said.

"Tell me if I'm right. When you hear what the teacher says, or when you study on your own, you are constantly changing what you see into creative images."

"What? I don't understand," he responded.

"OK. Let's say the teacher is talking about decimals in math, and that reminds you of *decibels* in your music—how loud you are playing your guitar—and that makes you think of the song you are working on, so you miss the whole point of what the teacher is explaining," I said.

"Well, yeah." Bill said. "That happens a lot."

"Even when you are studying for science or social studies, you probably picture something related to the topic and remember what you pictured and forget why you made the connections," I explained.

"All the time!" he said.

"What if you found out that you could use your ability to make connections to make learning easier?" I asked.

"That would be great," Bill said.

With a little practice, Bill gradually became reflectively aware of how his mind was metaphorically interpreting information. He admitted that one of the reasons he goofed off in class was because all these funny things kept popping into his mind and kept him from concentrating. Because he rarely input or processed the information presented by his teacher, his assignments and homework didn't make sense, so he didn't do them. This combination led to confusion, frustration, and inappropriate behavior.

To help him become aware of his need to focus and gather relevant information, I had him bring his textbooks and assignments to his sessions with me. With each activity, I asked him, "What do you see?" After he described or read the information, I asked, "What do you notice?" Then I asked Bill to tell me in his own words what he understood by the directions or information. In a very short time, he realized that when he gathered all the information and followed directions, the work was suddenly more interesting and easier to do. He began to consciously use his metaphorical thinking to understand and remember information. He was excited to realize that he could use that ability to make learning fun and meaningful without distorting the original information.

A couple months later, I saw Bill in the hall and asked him how things were going. He smiled and said, "Now that I understand what the teacher is saying, I'm not goofing off. I actually turn my homework in on time! Feels good, too."

Suggestions for Practice

1. *After explaining something, ask, "What sense did you make of this?" or "What did you understand by this?"* Do not have the

students repeat what you said. Encourage them to use their own words and compare ideas to something else. This reveals their level of understanding and the kinds of connections they are making in their own minds.

2. *Go on a metaphor hunt.* Encourage students to notice when they are using metaphors and when they hear or see metaphors in the media or everyday conversation. Stories, newscasts, speeches, commercials, and everyday talk are full of metaphors.

3. *Encourage students to be aware* of when they are seeing with their eyes (physical evidence around them) and when they are seeing with their minds (interpreting evidence metaphorically). Help students understand the value of noticing and gathering sensory data while still encouraging them to make creative, metaphorical connections.

4. *Help students evaluate the appropriateness of metaphors.* Does the metaphor really represent the main idea through comparison, or is it misleading?

5. *Use metaphors to compare unfamiliar information to something familiar* by highlighting similarities. Metaphors can help clarify and extend meaning.

6. *Listen and show respect when students come up with far-out ideas.* They may be showing signs of genius. Encourage students to explain why and how they come up with their ideas. Sometimes it is easier for them to draw what they are thinking than to put their thoughts into words.

7. *Take a few minutes each day for students to quietly reflect on a beautiful or positive thought.* Do this at the beginning of class to help students become calm and focused or at the end of a day or class period to help students reflect on what sense they are making of the information presented. Provide an opportunity for students to write about or illustrate their beautiful thoughts. Model and encourage creative, insightful "wonderings" and questions.

The Spiritual Dimensions
of Learning

In training seminars, I ask teachers to close their eyes and imagine they are assigned to teach in a remote jungle location. They have the basic necessities of food, water, clothing, and shelter, and they know the language and culture of the students. However, they have no books, no curriculum, no paper or pencils, no supervisors, no tests, and no copy machines or technology.

After outlining this scenario, I ask, "Could you still teach?" Teachers spontaneously respond, "Of course!" Then I ask, "What are the critical elements of the teaching/learning process that have to be present?" I ask each of them to write a list of the critical elements of teaching and learning and then share their lists in small groups. After 10 minutes or so, we reconvene and compile a master list, which typically is similar to the one in Figure 9.1.

When we've discussed each item on our group-generated list, I point to the list and ask, "Which one of these can you hold in your hand?" Teachers suddenly have a moment of insight when they realize that the essence of teaching and learning transcends the physical and organizational issues that occupy much of their time and energy. This little exercise helps raise their awareness of the spiritual dimensions of learning.

Figure 9.1	The Critical Elements of Teaching and Learning	
Acceptance	Enjoyment	Multiple ways to share information
Caring	Enthusiasm	Patience
Commitment	Flexibility	Perseverance
Communication	Interactions	Personal relationship with students
Cooperation	Interest	Respect
Creativity	Knowledge	Trust
Curiosity	Motivation	

Each of us has a set of personal beliefs about spiritual matters. These beliefs are the basis of unspoken assumptions and biases that motivate actions, decisions, and thought patterns. Because there is such diversity among people's spiritual beliefs, this is an issue that teachers commonly sidestep, especially in the context of public education. But by not addressing this issue, we risk overlooking not only key impediments to learning but also important ways we might help particular students learn more effectively. In my work with struggling students, it has become very clear to me that what they believe and feel about themselves, the subject matter, and learning in general directly affects their cognitive development.

The Importance of the Intangible

As my training exercise demonstrates, sometimes it's the things we can't see that make all the difference. Students have an uncanny way of "seeing" the truth of a teacher's attitudes. They have an extraordinary ability to sense emotional, spiritual, or intuitive communication. If we want students to trust us and believe what we tell them, we must build a personal relationship with them; learning, creating, and changing involve issues of the heart, or spirit. Without a trusting relationship, what teachers say or do has little influence. Students can tell if we are really interested in them, and they respond based on their perceptions.

Tom's Penetrating Gaze

Since kindergarten, Tom, a 4th grader, had received special education services for a variety of disorders, including learning disability, a behavior disorder, attention deficit disorder, hyperactivity, and a speech and language disorder. The first time he came into my office, Tom eyed me suspiciously. He plopped into a chair, crossed his legs, and twisted the elastic in his socks around his nervous fingers. I spread an assortment of brightly colored blocks on the table between us as I casually introduced myself and started to explain what we would be doing. He gave the blocks a passing glance and then resumed looking at me as he continued to twist his socks.

Tom's gaze was so intense and focused that I stopped what I was doing, smiled at him, looked right into his eyes, and said, "You know, I like you." This comment caught him off guard. He blushed, looked down at his socks, and then immediately looked back at me. Because I am always trying to understand how students think and why they do what they do, I gently asked, "When you look at someone like that, what are you looking at?"

"I look behind the teacher's eyes," he said.

"What kinds of things are you looking for?" I asked.

Tom responded without hesitation, "I look to see if they're for real."

"Tell me more. Help me understand," I prompted him.

"Well, it's like, you know, I want to know if they really care . . . if they mean what they say . . . if they're not mean or fake. I want to know if they're real."

Teachers' underlying negative beliefs and feelings about problem students are often less well-hidden than we intend. Parents, too, sometimes make offhanded, negative comments that hurt students emotionally, psychologically, and spiritually. That hurt shows up in both academic performance and in behavior.

Carson: Words That Hurt

Carson was not a "behavior problem," but it was his behavior —withdrawn, disinterested, neglectful of his assignments—that raised an alarm. In elementary school, he had been full of energy and engaged with friends and activities. But at the start of his 6th grade year, all that had changed. Was it just difficulty adjusting to new surroundings? Months passed, and Carson's withdrawn behavior persisted. After a trip to the doctor ruled out a medical problem, Carson was sent to meet with me.

When I first meet with students, I sometimes ask them to draw a self-portrait. Carson was hesitant to even pick up the pencil. Slouching in his chair, he looked over at me and then dropped his hands in his lap. After a few moments, he began to speak.

"I was a twin," Carson told me. "My twin brother died when we were born. Last summer, my mom said I was the one who should have died."

I gently asked him to tell me more. "I don't know any more," he replied. "And I don't know why she said it. She was all mad. But I just keep thinking about it."

"Have you talked with your mom or the counselor about this?" I asked.

"No," he responded, looking at me sheepishly. "You're the first one I told."

Then I asked Carson if he would like some help dealing with this situation, and he smiled faintly and nodded yes.

With Carson's permission, I called his mother to discuss the incident. She was shocked and did not remember ever making such a remark. She left work immediately and came to school to talk with her son, apologizing repeatedly and assuring him how much she loved him. The school counselor worked with them and arranged family counseling.

This incident illustrated how, without being aware of it, teachers and parents can sometimes say something or do something that initiates an emotional block to learning. Clearly, emotions play a huge part in every aspect of our lives, including learning. However, emotions are just one aspect of the spiritual dimensions of learning.

Definitions: Body, Soul, and Spirit

Learning involves the whole person—body, soul, and spirit.

The word *spirit,* according to Webster's *New World College Dictionary* (2001), originates from the Latin *spiritus,* meaning "breath, courage, vigor, soul, life," or *spirare,* meaning "to blow," "to breathe." Webster's defines *spirit* as a person's life principle, which was "originally regarded as inherent in the breath or as infused by a deity" (p. 1382). Webster's defines *soul* as "an entity which is regarded as being the immortal or spiritual part of the person and, though having no physical or material reality, is credited with the functions of thinking and willing, and hence determining all behavior" (p. 1369). The *body* consists of a person's physical organs, functions, and structures. (See Figure 9.2 for a summary of these definitions.)

The body, however, is more than the sum of its parts. Researchers are constantly learning more about the intricacies and interdependency of cells, organs, and systems. For learning, students need to effectively use their physical senses to gather information from the material world and transmit the data to the physical brain. The quality of the internal representation of data depends on the quality of data provided to the mind for processing. It is important to model for students how to notice what is available to the senses and how to determine what sensory information is relevant. Research is revealing more about the incredible functions and capabilities of the brain and how the brain stimulates its own continued growth and development.

Figure 9.2	Definitions of Body, Soul, and Spirit

Body: Physical, material characteristics of a person including sensory data-gathering capabilities (sight, touch, etc.) and neurochemical activity of the brain and other organs.

Soul: Immaterial entity that serves as person's "touch point" or interactive coordinator between body and spirit. The soul has three elements:

1. *Mind:* Cognition, attention, reflection, visualization (imagination), sensory perception and interpretation.

2. *Will:* Conscience, judgment, motivation, character, attitude, purpose, values, and beliefs.

3. *Emotions:* Feelings, personality, intuition.

Spirit: Life force that creates, learns, changes. The spirit enlivens and transcends physical elements of body and operates through the soul. Metability is a function of the spirit.

The brain transforms physical sensory data into neural-chemical energy. The soul processes the transformed data and feeds it to the spirit.

The soul—mind, will, and emotions—interacts with the body and spirit. The mind uses visualization and reflective awareness to process and transform sensory data into mental representations. Because the senses are the mind's only means of accessing the outside world, students need training in how to gather sensory data. Once information is transformed into representations of external reality, the mind perceives and processes the information as internal reality. The mind, will, and emotions interact with the body and spirit and develop more capabilities based on the effectiveness of those interactions.

The mind uses cognitive structures to process data for meaning by making connections, organizing patterns and relationships, formulating predictable rules, and abstracting generalizable principles. The mind interacts with the emotions and will when processing information.

Emotions filter and color information while the mind processes it. Although emotions are generally believed to be related to the limbic system in the center of the brain, they can be regulated by the mind. Emotional regulation depends on the effectiveness of cognitive structures in processing information and the effectiveness of the will in making decisions. A variety of emotions can affect physical and cognitive functions. To enhance memory, students benefit from emotional engagement with information.

The will is constantly evaluating information and making decisions or judgments to accept or reject data based on mind-generated and emotionally influenced values, beliefs, knowledge, and experience. Students can benefit from learning about morals and virtues as part of the criteria they use for evaluating information. Striving to treat others as we want to be treated can be helpful as students make decisions about their actions and interactions. Being illiterate in moral values can be a handicap for students just as being illiterate in reading and writing is. This aspect of mediation is important to students' development and their contributions to civil society.

As much as we would like to think that we perceive objective reality, the fact is, all sensory information transmitted to the brain is processed in the mind, filtered through emotions, and evaluated or judged by the will. It is then transmitted to the spirit, which uses that data to learn, create, and change. The continual development of metability depends on

• How effectively the mind uses cognitive structures to gather, organize, and process information.

• How effectively the will evaluates information and makes choices about actions based on values and beliefs.

• How effectively the emotions are managed to enhance life and learning.

What happens in the spirit is not always visible on the outside; however, we can become more proficient at observing and interpreting external indicators of internal growth and development. Providing for students' spiritual well-being is just as important as providing for their physical and mental well-being. One of the most effective ways that teachers can support students' well-being is by being sensitive to ways the spirit interacts with the body and soul to generate concept motifs.

Concept Motifs

Concept motifs are abstract entities that embody the integrated processing of the mind, emotions, and will. Concept motifs are to the spirit what food is to the body. The soul—mind, emotions, and will—processes available data using cognitive structures to integrate prior knowledge and experience, values, beliefs, and emotions. Once a judgment is made about a particular bit of data, the input, processing, and output are synchronized into a concept motif. *Input* consists of gathering data from the senses or from prior knowledge and experience. *Processing* includes reflecting, visualizing, and using cognitive structures to organize data for meaning. *Output* formulates internal or external representations of the processed data using words, symbols, actions, drawings, and so on.

Concept motifs are permeated with values, beliefs, and feelings. Many times, instantaneous and intuitive judgments form motifs with very little input or processing. As we become more reflectively aware, we can more effectively use our cognitive structures and suspend judgment to carefully gather and process more data before forming concept motifs.

A student's concept motifs interact with each other to form dynamic composites, which continue to change and interact with other composites. Students simultaneously form multiple concept motifs consciously and unconsciously based on patterns of processing that develop over the years. For example, students who have made judgments and formed concept motifs based on negative experiences with math (e.g., "Math is hard") will tend to continue building a composite of motifs every time they encounter math. Judgments such as "I'm not good at math" or "I hate math" cut off input and form motifs based on little input of information. To change this pattern, students have to suspend judgment and gather more sensory data (e.g., observe and listen to an explanation about how to solve a math problem). Then they need to reflect on and visualize the information, use their cognitive structures to process it, and output evidence of their understanding. These new motifs, based on judgments like "Math is really fun," replace existing ones.

Students who grow up forming judgments without ever transmitting the output for feedback and verification are in danger of creating private theories that may be misleading or completely erroneous. Later in life they may not even be aware that they are still forming concept motifs based on limited childhood perceptions. When confronted with new information, they could very easily misinterpret it in light of previous judgments and contribute to additional misconceptions.

For example, one evening a 30-year-old friend and I were driving along admiring a beautiful sunset. In a sincere, simple tone, she said, "You know, I've always wondered what the sun really does when it goes down at night." I tried not to show my surprise and reminded myself that many people still hold to theories and misconceptions formed in childhood because they never sought other explanations. As adults, they just assume their motifs are true or are too embarrassed to ask for clarification. My friend was taught about the sun, planets, and universe; however, if what she heard as a child did not make sense, she probably came up with her own private theory about what the sun does at night. Students become confused when they encounter information that is contrary to existing motifs. Sometimes they try to force the new information into pre-existing composites, sometimes they simply reject the information as false or irrelevant, and sometimes they form new concept motifs and build new composites.

Paul: "Don't Send Me to the Orphanage!"

One evening, after putting my 5-year-old son, Paul, to bed, I was sitting in the living room watching TV. Before long, Paul came sobbing into the room. I put him on my lap and asked what was wrong. Through his heartrending tears, he asked, "Are you really going to send me to the orphanage?" I gasped and asked him where that came from. "I heard you on the phone saying you had made the arrangements! Please don't send me to the orphanage!" Paul cried.

It took me a minute to remember that Paul had recently seen the movie *Little Orphan Annie* and to realize that he had made a connection in his mind between a phrase he heard in the movie and what he heard me say on the phone about "making arrangements." He didn't know I was talking about arrangements for an art exhibit. As I comforted and reassured him, I thought to myself, "Thank God he said something!" This judgment Paul had made, based on limited information, might otherwise have been a source of insecurity and mistrust.

Too often, students keep their concept motifs to themselves. Because the information they take in is filtered through their personal values, beliefs, and feelings (which are, in turn, influenced by prior knowledge and experience), students make judgments and come to conclusions that seem real and logical to them but not to anyone else. Once they have formed a concept motif, they try to align or "fit" future information into this structure.

As a teacher with 25 students in a classroom, I can teach a lesson the same way for all, but each will form a different concept motif. For this reason, it is important to frequently ask, "What did you understand by what I said?" As I worked with Calvin, a 6th grader, he became aware of how he was forming concept motifs.

Calvin's Concept Motifs

All through school, Calvin had been picked on by other kids. He had few friends, hated doing schoolwork, barely passed each year, and dreaded each day of school. He was also a very bright young man who read voraciously and drew with imagination and skill.

Calvin was so nervous and withdrawn when I began working with him that he responded with grunts, shrugs, and one-syllable words or mumbled sounds. He was fidgety and scratched various parts of his head and body as we talked, rarely looking at me except for nervous, fleeting glances. However, I soon noticed how much he enjoyed doing interactive tasks with me and how good he was at problem solving. I pointed out his strengths and capabilities and explained how he could use his abilities in school. As Calvin's confidence grew and he began to unpack his fears and misconceptions, he explained his thinking. He said, "You know, when I was in 1st grade, I didn't know how to play the games the other kids played. And I didn't know the answers to the questions the teacher asked. So I decided I must be bad or dumb. And I was afraid to ask, because I was afraid I might be right."

Every time Calvin didn't know the expected answer to a question, his inner voice said, *"See how dumb you are? You don't even know the answer."* Each judgment formed another motif that reinforced his prior judgments. When he perceived a gesture, word, or interaction as a put-down, he said to himself, *"See, something's wrong with me. Nobody likes me. I must be bad!"* Through mediation, 11-year-old Calvin realized he was using the lens of his 6-year-old self, who had limited knowledge and experience, to interpret what he was seeing, hearing, and feeling. With this insight, Calvin was able to expand his frame of reference and process input to create different motifs. It wasn't long before he was playing football with the other kids, turning his work in on time, and tolerating school much better.

From day one, babies begin to form concept motifs based on their perceptions of the world. They form primitive theories about how things work. We need to encourage young children to share their questions and wonderings. Most students do not remember much from their early years because their motifs and foundational composites were being developed during this time. However, I have worked with many adults who began to realize that concept motifs they formed as youngsters affected them all their lives, especially if the concept motifs were associated with strong positive or negative emotions. This is one reason interaction with nurturing adults is so important during children's early years. When adults continue to use motifs of their childhood to filter input, to process, and to output information, they limit their development. Because individuals can see from a limited perspective, we need to encourage positive interactions and collaboration among students.

Just as it is never too late to develop cognitive structures, it is never too late to change the way we form concept motifs. Many times I have observed how developing cognitive structures lead to transformational metability. New concept motifs can help previously formed composites realign and synchronize with newly created composites. Denise, a 3rd grader, experienced this liberating transformation.

Denise's Prize

Denise hated school. Her mother reported that each day started with conflict, tears, and dread. Homework sessions each night were torture, often lasting three or four hours. Lately, Denise had begun complaining of stomachaches and arguing that she was too sick to go to school.

At 8 years old, Denise could not read and had been diagnosed as learning disabled in language. She also had difficulties with math and other subjects. Although she had received special education and remedial services since 1st grade, Denise continued to struggle. Her mother requested that I work with her to identify her capabilities. "I know she's not dumb," Denise's mom said, "but she is so frustrated that she can't learn."

During the interactive sessions, Denise and I focused on reflective awareness. Encouraged to be more attentive to what her senses were telling her, Denise was able to visualize information and develop more effective cognitive tools to make connections, find patterns, formulate rules, and identify generalizable principles. As she did this, she transformed how she input, processed, and output information to form different concept motifs. She experienced enjoyment and success as she found that she could read fluently and solve complex verbal problems.

When she started reading successfully, Denise looked up at me and said, "Do I get a little something for this?" I calmly told her that I didn't give prizes and that satisfaction and enjoyment were their own reward. The next day, as she developed even more proficiency in her reading, she said with great excitement, as if being tickled on the inside, "I'm getting that tingle again!"

We talked about how school was fun now and how she was teaching herself to read. She started to read the next sentence, then stopped and looked at me, and said, "I like the prize." Confused, I asked what she meant. "This!" she replied, gesturing with outstretched arms. "I get to keep all this forever! *It feels good!*"

Like so many other students that I worked with, Denise taught herself to read by using her cognitive structures to make sense of information. She was able to change the way she formed concept motifs, which helped her develop her ability to learn, create, and change.

A Self-Reflection Exercise

Acknowledging the importance of the spiritual dimensions of learning equips educators to address many of the underlying causes of learning difficulties and inappropriate behaviors. This awareness also enables us to access and use a powerful resource within ourselves and within the students we want to help. After all, our own beliefs, feelings, and values directly affect all aspects of our lives, including our relationships with students, our understanding of subject matter, and our effectiveness as teachers.

When I work with teachers, I like to share my personal beliefs and values and explain how these influence my thinking. I do not try to convert them to my views or change their minds; I simply challenge them to consciously examine their own personal values and beliefs and reflect on how these directly and indirectly affect how they think and act. Following are some of the big questions I encourage them to ponder:

- Who am I?
- Why am I here? What is my purpose in life?
- What is my relationship with God, with others, and with myself?
- How do my beliefs affect my life?
- How can I make the world a better place? Why should I even try to do that?
- What is right and wrong? Good and evil? How can I know?
- How can I treat others as I would like to be treated?
- What happens after death? How does that affect how I live and learn?
- What matters in life?
- Why do I need to keep learning? How does what I know affect who I am?
- What are the two or three things I say in my mind, to myself, most often?

Some people might think these issues have little to do with education. I contend that they are the driving force behind our thoughts and actions. As teachers, we are trained *what* to teach, *how* to teach, and *when* to teach, and we may even study *why* we teach. However, little time is devoted to examining the following question: *Who am I, as a teacher and a person?* When we reflectively align what we think, feel, believe, do, and say, we have less stress and more energy for teaching and learning.

Suggestions for Practice

1. *Be mindful of what matters in teaching and learning and in life.* Think about the critical elements of teaching and learning that have to be present if we are to be effective. Too often we get caught up in the busywork and the peripheral issues that take so much time and energy. When we recognize that some things matter more than others in learning and in life, we are better able to greatly reduce our stress by prioritizing what gets attention.

2. *Recognize that students listen more with their hearts than with their heads.* They are constantly looking behind our eyes, our words, and our actions to see if we are for real. Our genuineness builds trusting relationships that make mediation more effective.

3. *Believe that every child can learn.* What we believe and think about a child is reflected in how we act and what we say. Avoid offhanded comments that can be taken as put-downs or cause embarrassment. Be aware that even the way we look at a child communicates whether we believe in him or her.

4. *Study the interdependence of body, soul, and spirit.* It is important to nurture the whole child. Just as we provide for physical and mental needs, we should also provide for spiritual needs. The more we understand about how these parts work together, the more effectively we can help our students develop all aspects of their lives.

5. *Help students learn to use their senses to effectively gather and input data.* The quality of processing and output depends on the quality of input data. It is important to both model and encourage how to notice what is available to the senses and how to determine what is relevant. Encourage students to become

reflectively aware of what their senses tell them and to visualize the information for processing.

6. *Encourage students to be aware of the three elements of their soul*—mind, will, and emotions—and how they function. Students need to use their cognitive structures to evaluate information and regulate emotions. Positive use of emotions enhances learning and makes it more enjoyable. We can also help students use their own spiritual standards (such as the Ten Commandments or the Golden Rule) as a basis for making moral judgments.

7. *Become more aware of how the spirit uses concept motifs.* Because we become the composite of concept motifs that we create, we are constantly changing and creating our capabilities. We can develop more awareness of how we are forming concept motifs by constantly reflecting on how we process and evaluate information. There is no limit to what we can learn as we develop our metability.

8. *Reflect on personal values, beliefs, and feelings about spiritual matters.* When we ponder the big questions such as the purpose of life, our spiritual and personal relationships, and norms for making choices and decisions, we can improve our relationships and enhance learning. The more we align what we think, feel, believe, do, and say, the more consistent we are in dealing with others. Encourage quiet, reflective time to get in touch with yourself.

• • •

Appendix A: Lesson Plan Model for Cognitive Engagement

Cognitive engagement is key to the development of metability—the ability to learn, change, and create. In this appendix, I provide a lesson plan model designed to do just that (see Figure A). My colleagues and I have used this simple model with students from preschool through high school, with college students, with teachers, and with parent groups.

Figure A	The Lesson Plan Model for Cognitive Engagement

1. **Explore.** Students notice and gather sensory input.

2. **Describe.** Students make connections with prior knowledge.

3. **Explain.** The teacher clarifies and builds on student descriptions, introduces new concepts, and asks students what sense they are making of it all.

4. **Demonstrate.** Students analyze and integrate information to demonstrate understanding by applying it.

5. **Evaluate.** Students and teacher reflect on and evaluate the effectiveness of the lesson, how it could be improved, and what questions come to mind as a result of the experience.

Step 1: Explore

Begin by inviting students to gather and notice sensory input. Present items related to the subject being studied. These items can be tangible, such as artifacts students can see and touch, or they can be symbolic, such as pictures, directions for a worksheet, a piece of literature, words, or symbols. Ask the students to carefully observe the items and see what they notice. Have them spend a few minutes just silently gathering sensory information and thinking about what their senses are telling them. At first, students may try to guess what you want them to see. However, as they learn to trust their senses and realize that there is no right or wrong answer, they become like investigators— much more engaged, observant, reflective, and willing to share.

Teachers who use this method are amazed at how much the students notice on their own. Too often, students in traditional schooling situations sit back and passively wait for the teacher to tell them what to look at and what to do. Doing the exploration without talking encourages reflective awareness of multiple sensory inputs. The noticing can be totally open ended, or it can focus on a particular aspect of an item. We are tempted to tell students what they should notice instead of letting them experience the thrill of discovery. The more sensory data the students gather, the more information they will have for processing.

Step 2: Describe

The next step is to invite students to describe what they've noticed about the items presented. To give more students the opportunity to verbalize their thoughts and make connections with prior knowledge and experience, have them talk with a partner or in small groups before beginning a whole-class discussion. They might also write or draw these "notices." During this step, the students provide windows to how they learn. They demonstrate how they use their cognitive structures to make connections, find patterns, formulate rules, and make abstract generalizations. They let you know the kinds of words they use for thinking and communicating, their level of knowledge, and how they process information. It is also important to do more listening than talking. When we listen to students, they become more confident and willing to share their ideas.

Step 3: Explain

Now it is the teacher's turn to clarify and build on student descriptions, introduce new concepts related to what they have noticed, and ask what sense students are making of these concepts. This is the time for teacher talk or instruction. By using the students' vocabulary and grounding the new information in their personal experience, you will make it much easier for them to create connections, change their understanding, and learn.

Step 4: Demonstrate

Now it is the students' turn to analyze and integrate information to demonstrate their understanding. Invite students to apply new information by using it in a project, writing, drawing, presentation, or report. Ask them how they would use their own words to explain the information to other students. It is important for students to have some say in how they will apply the information to demonstrate their understanding. It is also important that the knowledge demonstrated is not just an imitation of what the teacher presented. As students use their cognitive tools to further process information, they are developing metability by creating new connections, changing their understanding, and learning more information.

Step 5: Evaluate

The lesson concludes with time for both teacher and students to reflect and evaluate. *Encourage students to discuss ways to assess the effectiveness of their learning.* How can they tell for themselves if they have learned by creating and changing their knowledge or skill? Even young students can learn to create a guide or standard for evaluating the quality of their own work. When we make them dependent on someone else's evaluation, we are not equipping them to set high standards for themselves. Self-esteem is based on competence. The more effectively students can teach themselves and evaluate their own learning, the more they invest in their own education and enjoy learning. As students and teachers reflect on and evaluate the effectiveness of a lesson, they need to also consider how it could be improved and what questions come to mind as a result of the experience that would stimulate further learning.

Important Reminders

1. *Provide opportunities for students to actively gather sensory data,* discuss what they notice, and explain and demonstrate their understanding of what you present in class.

2. During the lesson, *frequently ask, "What sense are you making of this?"* Encourage students to ask themselves this question.

3. *Analyze your lessons* to see how much of the work you are doing and how much the students are doing. Help students use lessons to enhance their cognitive structures and develop metability.

• • •

Appendix B: An Invitation to Become a Reflective Researcher

Now that you have read about cognitive structures and learned about metability, I invite you to become reflective researchers and help me learn more about learning. Too often we think research can be done only by so-called experts. You, who are living and working with students on a daily basis, have plenty of expertise and valuable insights, observations, questions, and suggestions to offer your fellow educators.

Maybe you think that you don't have enough training to do research. As I've seen proven again and again with students, a person becomes good at something by doing it. As a professional learner, you continue to develop expertise with cognitive structures through reflective awareness and visualization. Using your cognitive structures to process information makes them more effective and develops your metability. You have already learned a lot from the challenges of life. This is an opportunity for you to use your knowledge and experience to help others.

We have all watched in awe and delight as babies learn to walk, to talk, and to figure things out on their own. Each of you has noticed unusual or interesting events involving your students without realizing the significance of your observations. Maybe you have wondered what you can do to make learning more enjoyable, engaging, and meaningful for your students. As you document what you notice and reflect on it, you will be modeling the learning process and contributing to this expanding body of knowledge.

The Basic Steps for Beginning Reflective Research

It's likely that you are already conducting a kind of commonsense, intuitive research based on what works in your own classroom. Here are some basic steps to help you systematically collect and analyze your observations and experiences (see Figure B). As you try these practices, keep using your common sense and trusting your instincts when you feel something is important. In this kind of research, you are not trying to change someone else. You are really looking at what *you* can do differently to help students help themselves. You are also focusing on learning with and from students about how they learn.

Figure B	The Reflective Research Process

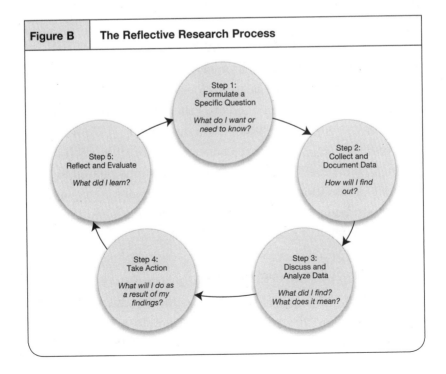

Step 1:
Formulate a
Specific Question

*What do I want or
need to know?*

Step 2:
Collect and
Document Data

*How will I find
out?*

Step 3:
Discuss and
Analyze Data

*What did I find?
What does it mean?*

Step 4:
Take Action

*What will I do as
a result of my
findings?*

Step 5:
Reflect and Evaluate

What did I learn?

Reflective research is cyclic. As you go through the steps, what you learn becomes stimulation for going through the steps again on a deeper level. Your research often starts with what appears to be the major issue, but as you investigate, you may find underlying issues that are causing it. As you penetrate each layer, you become aware of other issues you didn't realize existed.

Reflective research is also based on what I call the natural way of learning. It is the way infants and toddlers research to learn before they come to school and how older students learn when left to their own devices. It is the way most adults learn when confronted with something unfamiliar. This simple form of research yields valuable insights and is useful for many teaching and learning situations. Although these steps are listed in sequence, they may be used simultaneously. For example, you may be analyzing and discussing data while you are collecting it. The biggest challenge is keeping data organized. Let's look at those five basic steps in more detail.

Step 1: Formulate a Specific Question

Ask yourself: *What do I want to know or need to understand?* Start with something you have been wondering about or would like to see change. The question needs to reflect *your* involvement. For example, you might ask, "What happens when I ___ ?" "What can I do to improve ___ ?" "What causes me to react in such a way when ___ happens?" Start with specific questions related to your practice or situation. Although the issue or concern may appear to be a student's behavior, attitude, or learning, keep the focus on you and what *you* can do.

Step 2: Collect and Document Data

Ask yourself: *How will I find out?* Decide on the kind of data needed and how you will collect information about the issue, question, or problem. Set time limits. Gather data from multiple sources using methods such as observations, formal and informal interviews, surveys, photos and videos, records, schoolwork, drawings, e-mails, and so on. Write your observations and reflections as you go through this process. Your reflective notes become valuable data to help with analysis.

Step 3: Discuss and Analyze Data

Ask yourself: *What did I find? And what does it mean?* Reflect on and analyze data by organizing and classifying it, looking for cause–effect relationships, and comparing how bits of information are alike and different. As patterns emerge, you will begin to interpret your data to better understand issues relating to your original question. Talk to friends and colleagues about your findings and your preliminary interpretations. See if they see the same patterns you do or have other interpretations and insights. This is an important and enriching step, which gives you the opportunity to test your emerging theories and broaden your perspective.

Step 4: Take Action

Ask yourself: *What can I do, based on my findings?* Make a step-by-step action plan based on what you learned from your data analysis and guided by what you hope to accomplish in relation to your original question. Keep reflecting, collecting, and analyzing data while implementing the plan.

Step 5: Reflect and Evaluate

Ask yourself: *What did I learn from implementing my action plan? What worked well? What could I have done better? What do I still need to learn?* What you learn from your experimentation becomes the foundation for your next reflective research cycle as new questions emerge.

Important Reminders

When conducting reflective research, it is advisable to set a time frame, or the research can take on a life of its own and become unmanageable. I encourage novice researchers to start with "mini-projects." You might collect data for only a few hours and then analyze it, discuss it, and use it to create a simple plan of action. You might decide to collect data for a couple days or a couple weeks. After you analyze your data, design and implement an action plan. Keep it simple. As you evaluate the action plan, you begin to look at the next questions, and the cycle continues. This method can be used at home, school, or work or in any other real-life situation.

Reflective research is ongoing, self-directed professional development. It provides opportunities to collaborate in collecting and analyzing data to inform and improve practice. Reflective research is a way of thinking that develops our own cognitive structures and equips us to help our students develop theirs. The Lesson Plan Model for Cognitive Engagement in Appendix A can easily be adapted to stimulate students' reflective research:

• When students are exploring, encourage them to collect as much data as they can.

• When students are discussing what they noticed, encourage them to analyze the information in terms of relationships (e.g., similarities and differences, classifications, time and space).

• When you explain new information, encourage students to discuss what sense they are making of it.

• When students are demonstrating their understanding, encourage them to apply the information to real life.

• When students are evaluating their learning, encourage them to consider how they can improve or extend what they learned.

I invite you to become a reflective researcher and join me on this journey of learning about learning. You may want to start with

something as simple as documenting what happens when you explain something in class and then ask the students to write in their own words what sense they make of your explanation. Discuss and analyze your findings, then design an action plan to improve your instruction. As you continue to evaluate what you are doing, new questions will emerge to start the next cycle of reflective research. This process is both challenging and enlightening.

I am very interested in your reflections and analysis of how you use your everyday lessons to help students develop their cognitive structures and learn how to learn. Your questions, ideas, and insights are important to me and could possibly initiate a new direction in our research of learning. You can reach me at PO Box 692, Gig Harbor, Washington 98335, or via e-mail: bettygarner@yahoo.com.

* * *

Glossary

Cognitive structures are the basic mental processes used to make sense of information. Other names for cognitive structures include *mental structures, patterns of thought,* and *ways of thinking.*

Comparative thinking structures are foundational cognitive structures that enable a person to process information by identifying how bits of data are alike and different. They include *recognition, memorization, conservation of constancies, classification, spatial orientation, temporal orientation,* and *metaphorical thinking.* Comparative thinking structures are prerequisites for developing symbolic representation and logical reasoning cognitive structures.

Mediation includes interventions, such as interactive modeling, explaining, coaching, and questioning, that educators can use to help students develop cognitive structures.

Metability is an ongoing dynamic cycle of learning, creating, and changing. The word *metability* comes from *meta,* which means "change" (as in *metamorphosis*), and *ability,* which means "aptitude, capability, or capacity."

Reflective awareness means to thoughtfully consider information that we see, hear, touch, feel, taste, and smell. What we

notice, we process. Reflective awareness develops cognitive structures.

Reflective research is systematic, informal study of an issue, question, or situation. It includes identifying what to study, collecting and analyzing data, designing a plan of action based on data, and evaluating the plan's implementation.

Spiritual dimensions of learning are immaterial, intangible qualities or elements that permeate and influence all learning. Recognizing and acknowledging the importance of the spiritual dimensions of learning can equip educators to address many underlying causes of learning difficulties and inappropriate behaviors.

Visualization is the ability to mentally represent and manipulate information, ideas, feelings, and sensory experiences. To visualize, a person must be reflectively aware. Visualization makes it possible to do abstract thinking and planning. Visualization is not limited to mental pictures. It can also be mental sounds, mental feelings, and any other kind of verbal or nonverbal mental representation.

Resources

Barell, J. (2003). *Developing more curious minds.* Alexandria, VA: Association for Supervision and Curriculum Development.

Blagg, N. (1991). *Can we teach intelligence? A comprehensive evaluation of Feuerstein's Instrumental Enrichment Program.* Hillsdale, NJ: Lawrence Erlbaum.

Bruner, J. (2004a). *The process of education* (Rev. ed.). Cambridge, MA: Harvard University Press.

Bruner, J. (2004b). *Toward a theory of instruction* (New ed.). Cambridge, MA: Belknap Press.

Csikszentmihalyi, M. (1990). *Flow: The psychology of optimal experience.* New York: Harper & Row.

Csikszentmihalyi, M. (1997). *Creativity: Flow and the psychology of discovery and invention.* London: Harper Perennial.

Darling-Hammond, L., Bransford, J., LePage, P., Hammerness, K., & Duffy, H. (Eds.). (2005). *Preparing teachers for a changing world: What teachers should learn and be able to do.* San Francisco: Jossey-Bass.

Dewey, J. (1997). *How we think* (New ed.). Mineola, NY: Dover Publications.

Einstein, A. (2006). *Relativity: The special and the general theory* (Reprint ed.). New York: Penguin.

Feuerstein, R. (1979). *The learning potential assessment device.* Glenview, IL: Scott Foresman.

Feuerstein, R. (1980). *Instrumental enrichment: An intervention program for cognitive modifiability.* Glenview, IL: Scott Foresman.

Feuerstein, R., Klein, P. S., & Tannenbaum, A. J. (1991). *Mediated learning experiences: Theoretical, psychosocial, and learning implications.* London: Freund.

Gardner, H. (1983). *Frames of mind: The theory of multiple intelligences* (10th ed.). New York: Basic Books.

Gardner, H. (2004). *Changing minds: The art and science of changing our own and other people's minds.* Cambridge, MA: Harvard Business School Press.

Gardner, H. (2006). *Multiple intelligences: New horizons* (Reprint ed.). New York: Basic Books.

Gleick, J. (1988). *Chaos: The making of a new science* (Reprint ed.). New York: Penguin.

Gleick, J. (2000). *Faster: The acceleration of just about everything.* New York: Vintage Press.

Jensen, E. (2005). *Teaching with the brain in mind* (2nd ed.). Alexandria, VA: Association for Supervision and Curriculum Development.

Jensen, M. (2006). *Mindladder: Dynamic assessment and classroom learning.* Roswell, GA: International Center for Mediated Learning.

Kandel, E. R., Schwartz, J. H., & Jessell, T. M. (2000). *Principles of neural science* (4th ed.). New York: McGraw-Hill Medical.

Marzano, R. J., Pickering, D. J., & Pollock, J. E. (2001). *Classroom instruction that works: Research-based strategies for increasing student achievement.* Alexandria, VA: Association for Supervision and Curriculum Development.

National Research Council, Committee on Learning Research and Educational Practice, Bransford, J., Brown, A. L., & Cocking, R. R. (Eds.). (2000). *How people learn: Brain, mind, experience, and school* (Expanded ed.). Washington, DC: National Academies Press.

Perkins, D. (2001). *The eureka effect: The art and logic of breakthrough thinking.* New York: W. W. Norton.

Piaget, J. (1950). *The psychology of intelligence.* New York: Harcourt.

Piaget, J. (1954). *The construction of reality in the child.* New York: Basic Books.

Piaget, J. (1969). *The psychology of the child.* New York: Basic Books.

Restak, R. (2001). *The secret life of the brain.* Washington, DC: National Academies Press.

Restak, R. (2003). *The new brain: How the modern age is rewiring your mind.* New York: Rodale Books.

Restak, R. (2006). *The naked brain: How the emerging neurosociety is changing how we live, work, and love.* New York: Harmony Books.

Smith, L. M. (1968). *The complexities of an urban classroom: An analysis toward a general theory of teaching.* Austin, TX: Holt, Rinehart, and Winston.

Smith, L. M. (1988). *Explorations in ethnography: Vol 3. Innovation and change in schooling: History, politics, and agency.* London: Falmer Press.

Smith, L. M. (2004). Yesterday, today, tomorrow: Reflections on action research and qualitative inquiry. *Educational Action Research, 12*(2), 176–195.

Smith, L. M. (2005, June 10). *Reflections on qualitative inquiry.* Presentation at Action Research Collaborative (ARC), University of Missouri–St. Louis, St. Louis, Missouri.

Smith, L. M. (2006). The conception of reflective practice. *Perspectives in Education, 22*(2), 72–90.

Sousa, D. A. (2000). *How the brain learns* (2nd ed.). Thousand Oaks, CA: Corwin Press.

Sternberg, R. J. (2003). *Wisdom, intelligence, and creativity synthesized.* Cambridge, MA: Cambridge University Press.

Sternberg, R. J. (Ed.). (2004). *International handbook of intelligence.* Cambridge, MA: Cambridge University Press.

Tomlinson, C. A., & McTighe, J. (2006). *Integrating differentiated instruction and understanding by design: Connecting content and kids.* Alexandria, VA: Association for Supervision and Curriculum Development.

Underwood, G. (Ed.). (2001). *The Oxford guide to the mind.* New York: Oxford University Press.

Vygotsky, L. S. (2006). *Mind in society: The development of higher psychological processes* (M. Cole, V. John-Steiner, S. Scribner, & E. Souberman, Eds. & Trans.; New ed.). Cambridge, MA: Harvard University Press. (Original work published 1934)

Wadsworth, B. J. (2003). *Piaget's theory of cognitive and affective development: Foundations of constructivism* (5th ed.). Boston: Allyn & Bacon.

Webster's New World College Dictionary (4th ed.). (2001). Foster City, CA: IDG Books.

Wolfe, P. (2001). *Brain matters: Translating research into classroom practice.* Alexandria, VA: Association for Supervision and Curriculum Development.

Index

About the Author

Betty K. Garner is a professional learner who continues researching metability as a process of learning, creating, and changing. She received her Bachelor of Arts degree from Barat College in Lake Forest, Illinois; her Masters in Educational Processes from Maryville University in St. Louis, Missouri; and her Doctorate in Learning and Instruction from the University of Missouri-St. Louis. During her 40 years as an educator, she has served as a classroom teacher, art teacher, psychological examiner, professional learning coach, university instructor, researcher, and international consultant. She has been involved in numerous privately and publicly funded innovative professional development projects and continues to conduct seminars in her research, including an annual series of extended seminars in Europe. In the St. Louis area, she was a leader in facilitating candidates for National Board Certification, worked with adults who couldn't read, conducted hundreds of case studies with students struggling in school, facilitated workshops for parents, and trained teachers and administrators to become reflective practitioners and develop their metability. She is currently president of the Aesthetic of Lifelong Learning, a not-for-profit corporation designed to enhance the creative potential of educators, parents, and children.

You may contact the author at PO Box 692, Gig Harbor, Washington, 98335, or via e-mail: bettygarner@yahoo.com.

Related ASCD Resources

At the time of publication, the following ASCD resources were available (ASCD stock numbers appear in parentheses). For the most up-to-date information about ASCD resources, go to www.ascd.org.

Audios

Catching Kids Up: An Alternative to Remediation (CD) by James Riedl (#503272)

Implementing Brain Research (5-session CD set) by Robert Sylwester, Shana Kelber-Fisk and Lora Mosher, Keith L. Pentz, Beth Lipton, and Sharon Rowan (#507126)

Winning Over Challenging Students (8-session CD set) by Mark Ryan, Helen Teague, Lois Brown Easton, Susan Barton, Lesley S. Farmer, Carolyn Coil, Maryln Appelbaum, and William DeMeo

Books

The Best Schools: How Human Development Research Should Inform Educational Practice by Thomas Armstrong (#106044)

Developing Minds: A Resource Book for Teaching Thinking (3rd ed.) edited by Arthur L. Costa (#101063)

Developing More Curious Minds by John Barell (#101246)

Research-Based Strategies to Ignite Student Learning: Insights from a Neurologist and Classroom Teacher by Judy Willis (#107006)

Magazines and Newsletters

Classroom Leadership: Teaching All Students (entire issue, November 2003, #103392)

Educational Leadership: Closing Achievement Gaps (entire issue, November 2004, #105030), *Helping Struggling Students* (entire issue, February 2006, #106040), and *Understanding Learning Differences* (entire issue, November 2001, #101273)

Videos

Educating Everybody's Children (6 videos with 2 facilitator's guides) (#400228)

For more information: e-mail member@ascd.org; call 1-800-933-2723 or 703-578-9600, press 2; fax 703-575-5400; or write to Information Services, ASCD, 1703 N. Beauregard St., Alexandria, VA 22311-1714 USA.